Feudalism in Japan

STUDIES IN
WORLD CIVILIZATION
Consulting Editor:
Eugene Rice
Columbia University

Feudalism in Japan

PETER DUUS
Harvard University

Alfred A. Knopf *New York*

THIS IS A BORZOI BOOK
PUBLISHED BY ALFRED A. KNOPF, INC.

9 8 7 6 5 4 3 2

Copyright © 1969 by Peter Duus
All rights reserved under International and Pan-American
Copyright Conventions. Published in the United States by
Alfred A. Knopf, Inc., New York, and simultaneously in Canada
by Random House of Canada Limited, Toronto. Distributed by
Random House, Inc., New York.

Library of Congress Catalog Card Number: 69-15835

Manufactured in the United States of America

To Masayo

Preface

This essay deals with a problem that first caught my interest as an undergraduate and has fascinated me ever since: How and why did feudal institutions develop in Japan? It is not my intention to answer that question, but to introduce it to others in the hope that it might stimulate some of them to pursue a deeper exploration of the subject than time or knowledge have permitted me.

The reader will find the book is devoted to the institutions of feudal government in Japan. There may be some who object that the stress on feudalism as primarily a political and social phenomenon is an excessively narrow approach. I have not discussed economic developments nor the quality of moral life in premodern Japan, though both are fascinating subjects for comparative study. Rather, I have concentrated on the relations between the members of the warrior class and the institutions through which they exercised power. My reasons for doing so should be clear from the first chapter.

Being an amateur rather than an expert on feudal institutions, I have relied necessarily on the works of scholars who have made a deeper study of the subject. I am particularly indebted for an understanding of feudalism in Europe to the works of Marc Bloch and Joseph Strayer, for an understanding of feudalism in Japan to the works of Asakawa Kan'ichi and John W. Hall, and for an understanding of the difficulties of the comparative study of feudalism to the work of Rushton Coulborn.

PETER DUUS
Tokyo, Japan

Contents

Introduction xi

Chapter 1   What Is Feudalism? 3

Chapter 2   From Tribal Rule
             to Civil Monarchy 13
             Sixth-century Japan 14
             The Emergence of a Centralized
             Monarchy 20
             The Growth of the Aristocracy 25
             The Estate System 29

Chapter 3   From Civil Monarchy
             to Warrior Rule 35
             The Local Warrior 36
             The Political Emergence of the Warrior
             Chieftains 43
             The Establishment of the Kamakura
             Bakufu 48
             The Consolidation of the Bakufu 52

Chapter 4   From Warrior Rule
             to Feudal Anarchy 57
             The Decline of Bakufu Authority 58
             The Decline of the Estate System 62
             The Rise of the Provincial Constable 64
             The Daimyo at War 69
             The Daimyo at Peace 75

Chapter 5   From Feudal Anarchy
             to National Unity 81
             Reunification 82
             The Edo Bakufu 87

The Growth of Bureaucracy   *94*

The Freezing of Society   *99*

The Abolition of Feudal Forms   *104*

Bibliography   *109*

Chronology   *113*

Glossary   *115*

Index   follows page *116*

Introduction

Most early writers of universal history adopted one of two tactics: they wrote the story of their own civilization and called it a history of the world, or they wrote theological history, the story of how God ruled his earthly kingdom. Medieval Western historians did both at once. They identified their own past with the history of the human race and gave it meaning and value by believing that this past was the expression of a providential plan.

Early efforts to write universal history failed because mankind had no common past. The pre-Columbian civilizations of America attained their splendor in total isolation from the rest of the world. Although the many different ancient peoples living around the Mediterranean were often in close touch with one another, they had little knowledge about civilizations elsewhere. The Chinese knew accurately no other high civilization. Until the nineteenth century, they regarded the ideals of their own culture as normative for the entire world. Medieval Europe, despite fruitful contact with the Islamic world, was a closed society.

The fifteenth-century European voyages of discovery began a new era in the relations between Europe and the rest of the world. Between 1600 and 1900, Europeans displaced the populations of three other continents, conquered India, partitioned Africa, and decisively influenced the historical development of China and Japan. The expansion of Europe over the world gave Western historians a unifying theme: the story of how the non-Western world became the economic hinterland, political satellite, and technological debtor of Europe. Despite an enormously increased knowledge of the religions, arts and literatures, social structures, and political institutions of non-Western peoples, Western historians wrote a universal history that remained radically provincial. Only their assumptions changed. Before 1500, these assumptions were theological; by the nineteenth century, they were indistinguishable from those of intelligent colonial governors.

The decline of European dominance, the rise to power of

hitherto peripheral Western countries such as the United States and the Soviet Union and of non-Western ones such as China and Japan, and the emergence of a world economy and a state-system embracing the planet have all created further options and opened wider perspectives. Historians of the future will be able to write real world history because for good and ill the world has begun to live a single history; and while this makes it no easier than before to understand and write the history of the world's remoter past, contemporary realities and urgencies have widened our curiosity and enlarged our sympathies, made less provincial our notion of what is relevant in the world's past, and taught us to study non-Western civilizations with fewer ethnocentric preconceptions. One of the intellectual virtues of our time is the effort to combine a conviction of the relativism of our own past and present beliefs with an affirmation of the civilizing value of the study of non-Western cultures. Among teaching historians good evidence of this commitment has been the wish to include non-Western materials in the traditional Western Civilization survey course and the growing interest in teaching World Civilization.

Professor Duus' book on Japanese feudalism is one in a series of twelve paperbacks to be published under the title *Studies in World Civilization* that will help teachers to use non-Western studies in their civilization survey courses. One study will be devoted to modern Japan. There will be ten other studies in the series. One book is devoted to early and one book to modern developments in Africa, China, India, Latin America, and the Middle East.

History is long; the academic year lasts about thirty weeks. This disparity is one reason why survey courses tend to devote most of their time to studying the past of our own Western Civilization. The same disparity suggests the desirability of approaching non-Western history on a comparative basis. Professor Duus' book illustrates brilliantly the double advantage of this procedure: it is at once an admirable introduction to premodern Japanese history and a useful supplement to any study of European feudalism. Professor Duus' analysis of the word feudalism and his use of it in a non-European context clarifies one of the most interesting and difficult of historical terms. He points out the similarities of the *daimyo*, a Japanese feudal magnate, to the baronage of the European Middle Ages as well as the important differences between them. He contrasts Japanese political institutions between the thirteenth and sixteenth centuries with feudal government in Europe. Both his comparisons and his contrasts instruct. They make a formative period in Western medieval history more intelligible, and they make vividly accessible the less familiar contours of an elegant and martial society of East Asia.

Eugene Rice
Columbia University

Feudalism
in
Japan

Chapter 1

What Is
Feudalism?

The term "feudalism" belongs to that special class of words historians use to distinguish one complex historical situation from another. Such words are indispensable to the growth of historical knowledge. If historians did not use terms like "nation," "democracy," "revolution," "totalitarianism," and so forth, the writing of history would seem a mere recital of events without much sense or order. Historians would also be deprived of many insights into the working of human society. Such words, of course, are abstractions. But they are not *a priori* constructs spun out of the heads of metaphysicians. Rather, they are abstractions rooted in empirical observation. The historian could no more talk about "nations" if there were no concrete political units like New Zealand, Nigeria, and Nepal than a biologist could talk about "mammals" if there were no animals like mice, marmots, and monkeys. The general terms of the historian, like those of the biologist, are arrived at by a process of inductive thinking.

Few historians, however, are likely to agree on the precise meaning of most of these general terms. The difficulty arises partly because such words are not only technical terms, but are used in common parlance as well. Frequently the historian, without really thinking, uses such general words as the ordinary layman in his own society might. The result is endless confusion. A citizen of the Soviet Union could easily agree with a citizen of the United States on what a "mammal" is, but he would have considerable difficulty finding common ground on the meaning of "democracy." What the American might describe as "democracy" might be dismissed by the Soviet citizen as "bourgeois dictatorship." Conversely, the Soviet citizen might laud as "democratic" a political system the American might regard as "totalitarian." Even in our own society, the meaning of the word is quite elastic. A spokesman of the Students for a Democratic Society might be as vehement in his defense of democracy as an orator at an American Legion convention, but both are likely to have something quite different in mind. It is little wonder that historians are not able to settle the difficulty among themselves.

At the same time, most of the general terms the historian uses are concepts abstracted from a relatively limited number of cases. Nature supplies the biologist with a wealth of specimens to examine before he determines how best to define the category "mammal." But the historian has no such luxury. He therefore has to exercise a greater degree of arbitrariness in deciding which characteristics of a particular category of people, institutions, societies, or events are the most salient and which are only incidental. What should the historian include in the meaning of the term "revolution"—the use of violence, the overthrow of a *de jure* government, the substitution of one set of political institutions for another, the supplanting of one kind of class domination for another, or what? His answer will probably depend on whether he is most familiar with the French Revolution or the American Revolution, the Russian Revolution or the Chinese Revolution.

All these difficulties, plus some special ones, have plagued discussions of the term "feudalism" (and its French counterpart, *la féodalité*). Like most general terms used by modern historians, it is of relatively recent origin. It was not the product of the Middle Ages, which it purports to describe. William the Conqueror never announced that he was trying to impose "feudalism" on England, and doubtless he would have been puzzled if someone had told him that he was. It was only when men began to look back on the Middle Ages that the idea of "feudalism" came into being. The term was originally the creation of lawyers and antiquarians of the seventeenth century who used it to describe certain rules of land tenure, legal customs, and political institutions that had survived from medieval times to their own day and that were at curious variance with prevailing political ideas and practices. From these rather mild beginnings, the word took on less technical and more emotional connotations in the eighteenth century. Many of the laws and institutions described as "feudal" protected the privileges of the landed aristocracy and permitted them to exercise arbitrary powers over the mass of peasants. By the time of the French Revolution, feudalism was something associated with the bad old days, and ever since the words "feudal" and "feudalism" have retained this pejorative flavor. Even today, for example, an American liberal writing in a national magazine deplores the existence of a "feudal" landlord class in a South American country, or a leading Chinese Communist official in a speech before his party's Presidium calls for a struggle against "feudal reactionaries" in the countryside. Like its unfortunate partner "medieval," "feudalism" in common parlance has come to signify something backward, arbitrary, and even irrational.

Most historians do not use the term in this sense, but at the same time they are by no means agreed on what feudalism is. At one extreme are the Marxist historians, who see feudalism as a universal stage in human history through which every society must pass. For them the key element in feudalism is the exploitation of peasant serfs by a class of landowners to whom they are bound by custom and force and to whom they are compelled to provide labor or rent. In this view, which seems to be popular with some sociologists as well, feudalism is equated with a manorial or seigneurial economic system and the power structure that grows out of it. Using such a definition, Marxist historians have been able to find feudalism in such diverse societies as the great bureaucratic empires of China and India and the pastoral nomadic societies of Central Asia and the Middle East, as well as in medieval Europe. At the other extreme are many academic historians in France, England, and the United States who restrict its meaning to a much more narrow sense. They use it to describe a system of military and political organization in which armed warriors or knights rally to leaders who give them grants of land in return for personal service. Most of these writers regard feudalism not as a universal phenomenon but as a set of institutions peculiar to a limited area of Western Europe in the Middle Ages.

It would be tempting to conclude that historians, like Humpty Dumpty, feel that when they use the word "feudalism" it means what they choose it to mean—neither more nor less. There is an element of truth in this. The main reason historians find it so hard to agree on the meaning is that they so often use the word for different purposes. The Marxist, who is committed to the notion that there are certain laws at work in the evolution of human society, looks for universalities or total uniformities in history. Naturally he tries to stretch the category "feudal" as broadly as possible. The academic historian, on the other hand, is mainly interested in trying to distinguish what happened in medieval Europe from the classical civilizations that preceded it and the modern civilization that succeeded it. He is not concerned with showing that societies inevitably go through certain stages. He simply wants to point out the way the political institutions of Capetian France differed from those of Augustus Caesar or Louis XIV. He tries to be as precise as he can. Obviously there can be little meeting of minds among historians when they approach the problem of feudalism in such different ways.

If we are then to use the term "feudalism" at all, we should first decide what we want to use it for.

One important purpose the concept can serve is the study of comparative political history. The historian, instead of looking for universal stages in the history of man or trying to define what is unique about the experience of medieval Europe, can also raise the question of whether people outside European cultures ever found the institutions of feudalism a useful way of governing society. Certainly this has been true of other institutional patterns. The Chinese discovered the utility of bureaucratic rule as readily as the Romans did, and we are not surprised that bureaucratic states developed in both these cultures. Why should the same not be true of feudalism? This kind of question has not been neglected in debates over feudalism in the past: It was what the men of the eighteenth century were discussing when they spoke of "feudal" laws. Contemporary historians have touched on it as well, if only to make clear that they did not feel the question could be answered in a positive way.

But even if we decide to use the concept of feudalism in the study of comparative history, we cannot define the term in a factual vacuum. Like those engaged in the biological sciences, we have to build a model or a working definition of the term from some set of concrete data. Probably the best way to go about this is to look at the institutional arrangements of feudal Europe. Again we shall be following precedent. This is the best-known and first-studied example of feudalism, and the concrete case that gave birth to the term. It is also the model that most definitions of feudalism ultimately derive from.

What were the characteristics of feudal political organization in Europe between the tenth and the thirteenth centuries? First of all, feudal Europe was characterized by the absence of a strong centralized state. Government as we think of it today did not exist. There was no one center of power or authority that could claim the paramount and undisputed right to collect taxes, issue laws, raise armies, keep public peace and order, and dispense justice. To be sure, older traditions of central authority persisted in institutions such as the papacy, the monarchies, and the Holy

Roman Empire, but they were able to exercise political power only intermittently and only over relatively small groups of people. Effective government was fragmented into small local units, dominated by local feudal lords who performed most of the functions we normally associate with the state. The feudal lord, unaided except perhaps by a few trusted followers, was the only ruler most people saw or knew. It was he who maintained order, who settled disputes among men, and who determined what was law. In effect, public power was his private possession.

Second, the feudal lords of medieval Europe, as well as most of their followers and subordinates, were heavily armed, mounted fighting men. Together they constituted a kind of local aristocracy. The members of this warrior aristocracy were bound to one another by a peculiar set of social ties that gave them cohesion and established a rough order of prestige and authority among them. It was these ties that gave feudalism its essential character. The primary tie was that of vassalage, a personal bond of loyalty and obedience by which a warrior promised service to a lord or chieftain in return for military protection, security, and assistance. Unlike the ties of kinship or blood that characterize more primitive societies, vassalage was voluntary. At the same time, it was more personal than the loyalty that binds a subject to a monarch or a citizen to a modern state. Vassalage came closest perhaps to our idea of a contract, though it often rested on a warmth and a mutual respect not found in such a legal relationship. As feudal society came of age, the vassalage tie was often cemented by the granting of a benefice by the lord to the vassal in return for his service. In the early stages of feudalism, a lord might have supported a warrior in his own household or provided him with an office that gave him some income; but in its later stages, the benefice conventionally took the form of a grant of land or rights over land. This was the fief, or *feudum,* from which our term "feudalism" derives. For the vassal, the grant of a fief provided the leisure and the wealth necessary to maintain his status as a fighting man. For the lord, the fief served to reward the loyalty of the vassal and to guarantee his continued service in the future.

Finally, the maintenance of political power and the military ascendancy of the local feudal lord and his followers rested on their collective control over the land. Since trade and commerce were limited to luxury goods or commodities not easily found in the region, the principal economic resources of feudal Europe were the crops produced by the labor of the peasantry, who made up the mass of the population. Possession of rights over land gave the warrior aristocracy the authority to lay claim to these resources. Wealth and status were therefore measured in acreage, not in coin. As a result, feudal government became linked with the manorial economy. Fiefs were usually manors, which not only provided the warriors with sustenance and social status, but also gave them control over the peasant occupants of the land. Since land had such practical political and social value, vassals were anxious to secure as many manors as possible and lords were able to muster bands of followers by granting them. Most warriors were therefore seigneurs or masters of manors as well as fighting men. Their political and military functions, however, kept them from being mere landlords, a social type common to most other premodern agrarian economies.

Feudal government in medieval Europe was thus characterized by the absence of a strong centralized state, the devolution of political power into local political units or domains, the control of these domains by an aristocracy of mounted warriors linked by ties of vassalage and the fief, and a political economy in which land constituted the principal form of wealth. It would be a mistake, however, to think of this model as a static one. Like all human societies, feudal Europe grew and changed. The feudal France of Charlemagne (768–814) was significantly different in many ways from the feudal France of Philip Augustus (1180–1223). Feudal government was the product of a long evolution and in turn gave way to new political institutions over the course of several centuries. The motor for change was the continual search for a workable set of political institutions that would guarantee some measure of local order in a changing social and economic environment.

There were several phases in the development of feudal government in Europe. First came a long period of gestation, beginning in the first centuries of the Christian era, during which certain basic elements of feudalism (such as the use of personal vassals or retainers, the development of heavy cavalry as a technique of warfare, and the granting of land in return for service) evolved independently of one another. These practices were the product both of the late Roman Empire and of the primitive societies it encountered in Western Europe. Next came a period of experimentation when these practices or institutions were used in the service of a more or less centralized political regime; for example, in the late Merovingian and Carolingian states (ca. 650–900). By the tenth century, feudal government had reached a period of maturity often referred to as "high" feudalism. Feudal practices supplanted the last vestiges of centralized political organization as a means for preserving local order, and the local feudal domain became the chief political unit in society. This period, of course, corresponds most closely to feudal government as described in our model. Finally came a period of decline, when feudal practices were used to bring about the reestablishment of centralized authority in some form or other, usually as a national monarchy. In some parts of Europe, the decline proceeded more slowly than in others, but it was completed in most areas by the sixteenth century. Each of these phases shaded imperceptibly into the next, for feudal government was neither brought about nor overthrown by revolutions or the promulgation of constitutions.

Such, then, was the general outline of feudalism in Europe. Did a similar pattern of institutional growth take place outside Europe? In recent decades, historians have found "feudalism" in many parts of the non-European world, from the flood plains of the ancient Nile to the steppes of medieval Mongolia. On closer examination most of these non-European "feudalisms" prove to be more apparent than real. Sometimes the nature of the political institutions clearly does not fit our model; sometimes there is too little evidence to ascertain whether it did or not. But there is little question that the political institutions of Japan between 1300 and 1600 developed in much the same way as those of feudal Europe. Had a medieval European visited Japan during these centuries, he doubtless would have found much in Japanese society that resembled his own. Even Europeans of a later era, the missionaries and traders who arrived in Japan in the mid-sixteenth century, experienced a shock of recognition that they did not feel when they came in contact with other alien civilizations in Asia or the New World. They discovered intuitively what a wealth of historical and documentary study has confirmed since —that feudalism was not the unique invention of Europe but had been developed by the Japanese as well.

An examination of Japanese feudalism is not only interesting in itself; it also gives the historian a good opportunity to speculate on the origins and significance of feudalism in general. It is clear that the political institutions of feudal Japan and feudal Europe evolved independently of each other. Located thousands of miles apart across the Eurasian land mass, there was no possibility of direct influence between the two cultures. A comparison of the two is about as close to a laboratory experiment as the historian is ever likely to come. By sorting out the circumstances that led the medieval Japanese to adopt feudal political institutions, the historian can perhaps better understand why the medieval Europeans did so. He can perhaps also understand better the impact feudalism had on subsequent developments in the West. It is interesting to note, for example, that Japan was one of the first non-Western countries to borrow the modern political and economic institutions that emerged in Europe after the sixteenth century. Perhaps the Japanese were able to do so because they, like the Europeans, had gone through the feudal experience.

Of course, we should not expect feudal Japan to be a mirror image of feudal Europe, either in its pattern of development or in its institutional structure. The history of Japan was conditioned by a geographic, economic, social, and intellectual environment vastly different from that of Europe. What we should expect to find is a family resemblance, not an exact likeness. Equally important, we should not think of European feudalism as being more "normal" than Japanese feudalism. Building a model on the basis of the European experience is simply a convenience; close study of both Japan and Europe may mean that we will have to modify the model. It may be that some things we assume to be indispensable aspects of feudalism were not present in both cultures and that certain things we had not assumed to be so were in fact common to both. In short, we are still at the beginning of the comparative study of feudalism, and our definition of it will have to remain a fluid one.

Chapter 2

From
Tribal Rule to
Civil
Monarchy

The origins of Japanese history remind us very much of early European history. Like the gloomy forest lands of northwestern Europe, the mountainous Japanese archipelago did not provide a hospitable environment for the early development of civilization. It was a remote and backward region, regarded by the more advanced peoples of the North China plain as being beyond the pale of civilization. The inhabitants of the islands were a relatively primitive people who had learned the arts of pottery making, agriculture, and metalworking, but remained ignorant of writing or urban life. It was through contact with their more civilized neighbors that the early Japanese, like the early Europeans, were able to achieve a new level of cultural development. In Europe, Roman traders, armies, and colonists brought to the preliterate peoples of Gaul, Germany, and Britain the accumulated achievements of Mediterranean culture. Although never invaded by China, Japan experienced a similar development from the first century A.D. Initially through informal contacts and immigration of Chinese and Koreans into Japan and later through a conscious effort to borrow from China, the early Japanese adopted much of Chinese civilization to lay the foundation for a new civilization of their own.

One of the most significant lessons the peoples of both Europe and Japan learned from this cultural contact was a new way of organizing and ruling themselves. Into Western Europe flowed the Roman notion of a bureaucratic state ruled by law, and into Japan, the model of centralized monarchical rule. In both cultures, this new style of political organization had profound effects. The notion of a state manned by functionaries, protected by standing armies, and sustained by taxation helped dissolve the older bases of rule. The indigenous political leadership, which rested on magic, kinship, and hereditary rule, was unable to survive without considerable modification. Yet the new political order did not supplant the old one entirely. Neither the Japanese nor the Europeans were quite ready for the institutions of a centralized state. In Europe, once the Roman Empire had collapsed, the peoples of Gaul, Germany, and Britain were unable to make the apparatus of colonial administration work as the Romans had, and these institutions withered. In Japan, the political forms adopted from China proved much more durable, but they too lost their effectiveness as instruments of government. What resulted in both cultures was a synthesis of older indigenous social forms and the imported political institutions, a fusion that proved highly favorable to the growth of feudalism.

SIXTH-
CENTURY
JAPAN

Sixth-century Japan,* like Europe during the early phases of Roman expansion, was ruled by a tribal warrior aristocracy. Archaeological remains suggest their way of life was similar to that of the warlike nomadic peoples living in Manchuria, Mongolia, and

---

* Present-day Japan consists of four main islands: Kyushu, Shikoku, Honshu, and Hokkaido (see map). During the premodern period, most of the population was concentrated in the area stretching from northern Kyushu along both sides of the Inland Sea through the plain area around Osaka and Kyoto and along the Pacific coast to the Kanto region in central Honshu. Favorable agricultural conditions and convenient communications routes made this part of the archipelago most suitable for settlement. Most of the events described in this book took place in this section of the country.

14

more distant parts of Central Asia. Like these steppe peoples, Japanese warriors fought on horseback, armed with bow and arrow. They too carried long straight swords made of wrought iron and wore quilted clothing protected by light body armor made of hard leather or riveted iron slats. Whether this ruling class was indigenous in origin or descended from continental Asian invaders is a matter of some debate, but there can be little doubt that their ascendancy rested on military prowess. Moreover, the techniques of mounted warfare they had mastered foreshadowed the fighting skills of the feudal class that was to dominate Japan's premodern history.

Unlike the later feudal class, however, their social organization was a relatively simple one. They were bound not by feudal ties of vassalage but by real or imagined ties of kinship. The key social unit was the patriarchal clan (extended family), a loose cluster of conjugal families that claimed descent from a common ancestor. Often the claim of a common ancestor was not a biological fact. New families were frequently incorporated into the clans, and branches often split off to form new lines of their own. In any event, the tie of blood was the most compelling basis of social unity. The leadership of the clan units was likewise determined by blood. The clan chieftain was held to be the chief lineal descendant of the original ancestor, and it was he who presided over the worship of the totemic or tutelary deity that was regarded as the progenitor of the clan and the protector of its fortunes. At the same time, the clan chieftain was also a political leader who settled disputes among the members of the clan and who probably led them in time of war as well. As in many primitive societies, life was simple enough that the work of patriarch, priest, and ruler could be done by one man.

The clans of the warrior overlords varied greatly in size, but usually their members lived in a single region, and the geographical limits of the extended family probably corresponded to the natural lay of the land. The mass of the people who lived in these regions, however, did not belong to the families of the warriors and their chieftains. Rather, they were hereditary dependent serfs whose labor and services supplied the ruling class with its material needs. They were organized into groups called *be*, communities of workers engaged in the same occupation. The commoners were not thought of as being kinsmen of the rulers, but we do not know precisely how the sixth-century Japanese viewed their relationship. About all that can be said with certainty is that they lived in hamlets or villages side by side with their masters and that they worked as farmers, potters, weavers, sake brewers, fishermen, and the like, providing the masters with the crops or goods they produced as tribute or labor service. With its attached hereditary serfs the bailiwick of a local chieftain's extended family formed a highly self-sufficient local economic unit. This self-sufficiency was probably also enhanced by Japan's hilly topography, which divided the country into many small valleys, river deltas, and coastal plains and which made transportation difficult.

Although their social organization was no more complex than that of the earliest barbarian peoples of Western Europe, the economy of the sixth-century Japanese was perhaps more advanced. Agriculture, which centered on the production of rice as the main crop, did not depend on the vagaries of rainfall, as in Europe. For many centuries the peasant farmers of Japan had practiced irrigation and thus could feed a much denser population than could the rainfall agriculture of Europe. Many more people could be supported by an acre of rice-paddy land than by an acre of the wheat, barley, oats, or vegetable crops that formed the staples of the European diet. Irrigated rice cultivation also required more human labor. The plowing and planting of the seedbeds, the transplanting of the seedlings to the paddy, and the cutting of rice stalks in the autumn harvest all had to be done by hand. It was difficult to substitute the power of the mechanical devices, or even of draft animals, for the energy of human muscle. Because agriculture was labor intensive, most farming was done on small plots worked by a man and his family (Japan always had a more checkerboard landscape than Europe). At the same time, since cultivation of the land was dependent on irrigation, the Japanese peasant community was also a more tightly knit unit. Not only did all the inhabitants of a village work together at planting time, but the need to regulate the flow of water from one paddy to another, and the need for one hamlet to share the water of a stream with its neighbor, made the communities of cultivators much more dependent on one another than those of Europe. The great amount of labor needed to divert streams, to build irrigation ditches, and to raise dikes and walls between paddy fields also made it extremely difficult for an individual family to strike out on its own as could the pioneer settlers of early Europe. Geography and technology conspired to produce a stronger sense of communal interdependence in Japan.

Given the small, isolated, and closely knit character of the tribal community, the social horizons of most sixth-century Japanese were undoubtedly local. But there were also bonds that transcended the blood ties between clan members, the hereditary ties of dependence between the serfs and their masters, and the communal ties of interdependence among the peasant communities. Although it is difficult to speak of the existence of a centralized state, the shadowy outlines of a tribal monarchy had already emerged in western and central Honshu (see map). One of the earliest historical records of Japan suggests that by the late third or early fourth century a powerful warrior clan or group of clans living in the Yamato basin, an extremely rich and fertile plain in central Honshu, had subdued chieftains living in other parts of the country by a series of bloody wars. In the vivid words of the *Nihongi*,* these conquering groups had "clad

---

* The *Nihongi*, or *Nihon shoki* (*Chronicles of Japan*), was completed in 720. As a historical record it leaves much to be desired, for its compilers incorporated native myths into it, plagiarized passages from Chinese historical texts, and imposed an arbitrary chronology on actual events. Nevertheless, although it requires careful interpretation, the *Nihongi* seems to be relatively reliable as a historical account for the period following the fifth century.

themselves in armor and helmet and gone across hills and waters, [and] sparing no time for rest . . . conquered the fifty-five countries of hairy men in the east, and brought to their knees the sixty-six countries of various barbarians in the west." As a result of this conquest, the defeated chieftains acknowledged the hegemony of the chieftain of the Yamato clan. In the sixth century this paramount chieftain was called "the great lord" (*ōgimi*). Modern historians refer to him simply as the Yamato ruler.

Although the supremacy of the Yamato ruler had originally been won with the sword, his position was supported in more pacific ways by the sixth century. It was buttressed, first of all, by a sacred myth of legitimacy. The Yamato ruler claimed as his ancestor the sun goddess Amaterasu, the principal deity in the prolific and complicated Shintō pantheon.* As the chief living descendant of the goddess he enjoyed a sacerdotal position superior to the other clan chieftains, who had access to less potent gods. Second, the Yamato ruler also used the ties of blood and kinship to support his authority and power. Members of the ruling family were sometimes established as local chieftains, and clans not directly related to the Yamato ruler often sent their daughters or women to become the wives of the ruler or his kinsmen. Since polygamy was practiced, the Yamato court could accommodate a large number of spouses or consorts and presumably a large number of marriage ties with the local clan chieftains. Third, the Yamato ruler sometimes appointed lesser chieftains as local officials to preside over geographically defined administrative units that sent tribute to the Yamato ruler. Since these local officials were not born to their position but held

---

* Shintō ("the Way of the Gods") was the indigenous religion of the Japanese before the advent of Buddhism. It had no highly organized ecclesiastical system nor even a very elaborate set of beliefs. Worship centered on the offering of prayers and sacrifices to local agricultural deities, unusual natural objects considered to be holy, and the totemic ancestors of the clan aristocracy. Most of its rituals aimed at promoting the well-being of the community or society as a whole.

it at the pleasure of the ruler, we can detect here a rudimentary idea of a local officialdom. Similarly, other more powerful chieftains were appointed to serve as counselors to the ruler or as household officials to supervise the work of the hereditary serfs and artisans who served him. And finally, although the original founders of the Yamato line probably exercised direct control only over the people and land in the Yamato region and its vicinity, by the sixth century the ruling family had begun to appropriate land, granaries, and serfs in remoter areas of the country. Sometimes the incumbent ruler would designate certain groups of farmer serfs to send their produce directly to the Yamato court, and sometimes he would designate certain lands as hereditary holdings of branches of the ruling family.

Yet for all his primacy, the Yamato ruler in the sixth century was in no sense absolute, nor were his powers precisely defined. Aside from the people and lands regarded as belonging to the ruling family, the authority of the ruler extended only to the chieftains of the other warrior clans and not to the people and land under their control. The idea of the allegiance of all the people to a supreme ruler was still alien to Japan. Often local chieftains would defy the authority of the Yamato ruler; in 527, for example, a local chieftain in northern Kyushu (see map) interfered with an expedition planned against the Korean peninsula, and his revolt took several years to crush. Moreover, the personal authority of the ruler was frequently circumscribed by the powerful chieftains surrounding him. Owing to the lack of a fixed law of succession, there were several instances when chieftains interfered directly in the succession of the ruling family. Between 531 and 537, for example, there were two rival Yamato rulers, each backed by a rival faction of chieftains, and in the 580s several of the leading clans engaged in an open struggle for control of the ruler. The country lacked a sense of unity, the concept of legitimate public authority, and the administrative techniques by which such authority could make its demands felt. In short, the sixth-century Japanese had still not discovered the idea of the sovereign state.

It was doubtless to strengthen the power of the Yamato ruler that, beginning in the early seventh century, the Japanese embarked on a mass importation of Chinese political ideas, administrative practices, and governmental institutions. In part, this borrowing may have been prompted by the reunification of China under the Sui and T'ang dynasties. The revived Chinese state, which brought order to China after nearly four centuries of divisiveness, seems to have impressed the Japanese as much as it did many other peoples on China's borders. Certain chieftains close to the Yamato ruler, as well as members of the ruling family itself, saw in the Chinese model a pattern on which to consolidate the power of the Yamato ruler. China provided both a political theory and a set of political institutions that went far beyond the crude and tentative attempts at centralization begun in the sixth century. In the space of a hundred years, starting with the limited reforms of Prince Shōtoku (573–621), a brilliant scion of the ruling family who served as regent for his aunt, and ending with the promulgation of comprehensive Chinese-style legal codes in the early eighth century, reform elements at the Yamato court reshaped the entire political structure of the country.

Basic to the innovations of the seventh and early eighth centuries was a new concept of the ruler. The reformers borrowed the Chinese notion of an absolute monarch whose authority transcended the ties of kinship. This new concept of monarchy, which was first embodied in the Seventeen-Article Constitution attributed to Prince Shōtoku and later reiterated in the reform edicts of the mid-seventh century, envisaged a single center of sovereignty within the country. The monarch or emperor (*tennō*) was regarded as "the master of the people and the master of the whole land," and the people were to give their allegiance only to him. He was not to be at the mercy of his powerful subjects or a pawn in their struggles, as the Yamato ruler had often been, but was to rule with the aid of wise and able ministers who would be appointed at his will and who would place loyalty and service to him above their own selfish interests. It is easy to see why this conception of a bureaucratic monarchy appealed to the reformers of the seventh century. In place of a country divided among a welter of contentious local chieftains, it substituted the promise of an orderly and harmonious society in which the people accepted the leadership of their superiors and officials behaved with decorum. At its base lay the vision of a public power that would transcend localism and disorder and would ensure the common good of all.

The theories of legitimacy that accompanied the new concept of monarchy were more sophisticated than the Yamato ruler's claim to divine descent from the Sun Goddess. These theories were both Buddhist and Confucian in inspiration. From Confucianism came the notion that the world of man and the world of nature were intimately linked. If human society was out of joint, the world of nature would be similarly afflicted. Floods, earthquakes, plagues, and famine were not chance events, but the consequence of disunity and disharmony among men. The function of the ruler was to preserve order in human society so that the cosmic balance could be maintained. From Buddhism came the notion that the ruler was to be the protector of religious faith. Were the monarch to reverence the teachings of Buddhism and to spread them among his people, not only would peace and harmony result from the spread of Buddhist morality, but the Buddha would bestow his special blessings on the ruler. Both these notions were grafted to the myth of the ruler's divine ancestry to produce a far more potent sanction for his authority.

It was one thing to claim new powers for the sovereign and to justify them, but quite another to give them force. To accomplish this, the reformers of the seventh and eighth centuries quickly adopted the idea of written law, using as their guide the legal codes of the T'ang dynasty. The introduction of written law had a dual impact on the political organization of the Japanese. On the one hand, it meant that ties between men were no longer governed simply by custom; the written word was substituted for fallible human memory. The powers of the ruler, the duties of his ministers, and the obligations of the people were recorded in a form that could be transmitted over generations, and any changes in these fundamental relations would be embodied in new written laws. Codification of these relations perhaps gave a greater stability to the basic institutions of government. On the other hand, the written codes extended the ambit of the ruler's authority. Because written documents or orders issuing from the sovereign had as great a claim to obedience as the sanctions of magic, the obligations of kinship, or the threat of force, it became much easier to hold together a large number of people over a wide territory without resort to face-to-face contact or direct personal relations. Written law, in short, made possible a greater degree of government by remote control.

By the early eighth century, the effort to draft legal codes for Japan culminated in the Taihō Code of 701 and the Yōrō Code of 718. Each consisted of two main sections: a detailed penal code defining crimes and punishments, and an administrative code defining and regulating offices of state. The latter is perhaps of greater interest to us, for it established the apparatus of the bureaucratic state that was to support the rule of the monarch. At the center of this apparatus was an elaborate structure of central ministries and bureaus modeled on that of the T'ang empire. Officials in these bodies were appointed by the emperor, who also had the power to grant or withdraw court rank, the key to official position. Officials could be removed if disloyal, rewarded if hard-working, and shifted through a series of posts at the behest of the ruler. The central bureaucracy was housed in a permanent capital city, a visible embodiment of the power of the monarch. Laid out on a symmetrical grid pattern, it symbolized the orderly and harmonious character of imperial rule. The emperor's palace was located at the northern end of the city, and close by were the buildings of the central offices and ministries. Surrounded by a wall and moat, the city was a small-scale reproduction of the imperial capitals of China. The first site of the capital was at Nara (established in 710), but in 794 it was moved to Heian, later known as Kyoto (see map), where it remained until the nineteenth century.

The maintenance of the emperor, the capital, and the central bureaucracy was, of course, expensive. The reformers therefore introduced a system of land distribution and tax collection to provide the new state with revenue. Since the emperor was the "master of the land of the country," all rice fields were regarded as public land which the emperor had the right to grant to his subjects. Probably from the middle or late seventh century, the imperial government began to carry out censuses of the peasantry and to survey the cultivated rice land within the country. Once surveyed, the land was divided into fields of roughly equal extent and assigned to peasant families according to their size. The larger the family, the larger the allotment it received. The purpose behind this "mouth-share field" system was to provide each family with enough land to feed its members. To be sure, such a massive rearrangement of land tenure could not be accomplished all at once, and it seems to have taken place over several generations.

Since land was public, it could not be bought or sold or otherwise disposed of by the peasant cultivators. They did not own the soil, they only had the right to use it. Every six years the land was redistributed to make sure that allotments still corresponded to the population. New censuses were taken to ascertain changes owing to deaths or births, and lands were reassigned on the basis of the new census registers. In return for the right to use the land, the peasants were obliged to pay taxes in rice, in labor, or in some local product that could be easily transported to the capital or to the headquarters of the local official. This system transformed the peasantry from hereditary dependents of local chieftains to serfs of the state and linked them directly to the central authority of the imperial government.

Such an elaborate system of land distribution and taxation could be no better than the machinery devised to administer it. The new state rested on a centralized system of local government. In place of the vaguely defined territories of the sixth-century clans, the country was divided into sixty-six provinces, each of which was subdivided into a large number of districts. The provinces were administered by provincial governors appointed by the central government to supervise the collection of taxes and the execution of imperial edicts and laws. These officials lived in provincial capitals that were small-scale physical replicas of the national capital. But the centrally appointed officialdom ended at the provincial level. Below were the district chieftains, appointed not by the capital but by the provincial governors. It was they who held the key to effective administration of the country, for in their hands lay the power to collect taxes directly from the peasantry, to keep local records, and to settle disputes over land. For the mass of the peasantry it was the district chieftain who represented the authority of the government. The efficient functioning of the imported bureaucratic model depended on the chieftains' honesty, their loyalty to the state's interest rather than their own, and their ability to carry out the commands of the central government.

Finally, the reformers attempted to buttress the imperial government with a new style of military organization. The emperor was not to be dependent on uncertain alliances with local clan chieftains. Like its counterpart in China, the new state was to have its own standing army. Three separate bodies of guard units were established at the capital, but more important, local army units were created in the provinces as well. These local garrisons, housed in each of the provincial capitals, were recruited from the able-bodied men of the province. Military service, like the payment of taxes, was part of the obligation the peasantry bore in return for the use of rice land. A locally recruited militia of peasant soldiers, moreover, was more likely to defend its own lands than an army of professional troops. In addition to these provincial garrisons, permanent garrisons were established in certain key areas, especially along the frontier in the northeastern part of Honshu (see map), to subdue or keep in check the "barbarians" who remained outside the capital's political control. These outposts were similar to the military border colonies in China that defended the country against the peoples of Central Asia.

THE GROWTH OF THE ARISTOCRACY

The idea of a monarchical state ruled by public officials dedicated to the welfare of the people and loyal to the sovereign did not survive in practice much beyond the eighth century. To be sure, the institutions established by the seventh-century reformers were not suddenly swept aside. Rather, they were eroded by older habits of thought and social behavior. Though early reformers like Prince Shōtoku seem to have conceived of making Japan into a bureaucratic monarchy run by officials, their efforts produced an aristocratic monarchy based on nobility of birth, different in form but often close in spirit to the old clan system. Political power was no longer decentralized as it had been before the reforms took place. Prestige, wealth, and authority were concentrated at the capital rather than dispersed throughout the country. But old habits of mind, particularly the idea of hereditary power and the importance of blood ties in determining loyalty, eroded the newly imported concept of public power and profoundly modified the operation of the new institutions that embodied it.

In adapting the Chinese system of government to native conditions, the reformers had left out one essential ingredient: bureaucratic ability. In China, recruitment and selection of public officials were determined largely by an examination system. "Men of talent" were selected by fixed standards of literary skill and character to fill official posts. The Japanese paid lip service to this principle by setting up an elaborate system of government schools and examinations, but in practice access to these schools as well as to public office was limited to those who held court rank. Only a person who belonged to the hereditary rank-holding class could hope for office.

Part of the reason for this modification of the Chinese practice may have been that the reformers never really understood the rationale of the examination system. But other practical considerations were probably more important. The Japanese state had been reshaped in the seventh century mainly by persuasion, not by force. Although there had been violence during the Taika coup d'etat of 645, and the Jinshin disturbance of 672 under the reign of the Emperor Kōbun, these were minor episodes considering the extent of the changes wrought in the country. Whether by choice or by default, the reformers surrounding the throne did not feel themselves strong enough to destroy the old local chieftain class or deprive them of their privileged position in society. Instead, they recast old powers and privileges into new forms.

Many of the clan leaders, particularly those traditionally close to the Yamato ruling family and hence most loyal to it, were converted into a hereditary nobility by the grant of court rank. The possession of rank entitled them to offices in the central government that brought with them considerable sources of wealth. In lieu of a salary, officials were assigned lands, household servants, and serf laborers to provide for their maintenance. They were also free from the obligation to pay taxes (see page 30). Local chieftains of lesser status or from more remote areas were likewise rewarded by the central government. Those who did not receive court rank or office were often appointed to some local post, perhaps as district chief or as subordinate official in the provincial official hierarchy. It made sense to appoint such men because traditionally they already held power in the local areas. The old clan leadership was thus converted into a new ruling class, one whose social and political position were dependent on imperial authority, but whose economic position was often no less advantageous than it had been in the days before the reforms took place.

Despite these continuities, however, the introduction of the new system had created a profound gap between the capital and the provinces. Life in the capital, toward which the tax revenues of the country flowed, far outshone the provincial centers in wealth, culture, and grandeur. Within a few generations, the descendants of the clan chieftains who had remained in the countryside had not only lost the independence of action and the monopoly of local prestige that their forefathers possessed, but had fallen in the social hierarchy relative to the aristocrats who dominated the posts in the central government. By the tenth century, the brocaded courtiers at Heian regarded a marriage tie with a provincial family as a misalliance, and a somewhat embarrassing one at that. Viewed from the comfortable vantage point of the capital, the provinces were remote, even forbidding, backwaters bereft of amenities and cultural brilliance.

Secure in their wealth and position, the imperial family and the leading aristocratic families surrounding it became less and less interested in the practical functions of their offices. The emperor was no longer a public figure wielding the legal powers of the monarchy with decisiveness and assurance. Often emperors were children or young men whose main function was to preside over official ceremonies and religious rituals. Frequently, to escape the tedium of his duties, the emperor would abdicate at an early age, and another child monarch would be chosen to replace him. As a result, the legal powers of the emperor were usually exercised by his advisers or counselors. From the mid-ninth century, the heads of the powerful Fujiwara family, who cleverly married their daughters into the imperial family, assumed the posts of regent (*sesshō*) and chancellor (*kampaku*) and exercised real control over the imperial court. When their influence declined in the mid-eleventh century, the abdicated emperor (who took the title of retired or cloistered emperor) usually served as the power behind the throne, dominating the infant heir who succeeded him. Direct imperial rule remained an ideal, but it was more honored in the breach than in the custom.

The bureaus and ministries of the central government similarly became fossilized. Members of aristocratic families continued to compete for office in order to secure income and to enhance their prestige at court, but the imperial prerogative of appointing officials gradually fell into disuse. From the ninth century rank and office were often sold to nobles hungry for more land or greater prestige. Many posts became the hereditary preserve of the heads of certain aristocratic families. Naturally this meant that important posts were often held by persons obviously not competent to perform the duties required by the administrative codes. In the early eleventh century, for example, the Chief of Imperial Police, assigned the task of keeping peace at the capital, was a sixteen-year-old boy. Official activities became ritualized, completely formal in character. Ceremonies originally intended to serve some practical role, such as the installation of new officials, the reporting of the number of fields on which no harvests had been taken, or the rounding up of criminals in the capital, became occasions for elaborate banquets governed by a rigid and stifling code of etiquette. The practical work of the state was taken over by more informal bodies that grew up outside the legal codes or by household officials of powerful aristocratic families.

The decline of aristocratic interest in the functioning of the central government was accompanied by a declining concern for provincial affairs. Though provincial governors had been regularly dispatched and rotated by the central government during the early days of the new system, this practice fell into disuse at the end of the ninth century. Provincial governorships became titular posts, sinecures like the offices in the central government, and were often held concurrently with other posts as a source of income. Aristocrats appointed to governorships would handle provincial affairs through stewards of their own households or through personal deputies dispatched to the provinces. Consequently, provincial administration became much more lax. Though the provincial governments continued to levy labor conscripts and send tax revenues to the capital, the carrying out of land surveys, the periodic censuses, and the regular redistribution of rice lands were abandoned. Provincial officials and district chieftains increasingly exploited their positions for personal ends rather than for the benefit of the central government. They would use the labor corvée to clear lands in their own name, hold back tax receipts instead of sending them to the capital, force peasants to borrow rice seed from the provincial granaries in return for exorbitant interest rates, and so forth. Just as the central government became fossilized, the provincial governments became riddled with corruption, local officials misappropriated state revenues, and the local populace was exploited for private ends.

THE ESTATE SYSTEM
Despite the radical departure of the monarchical state from the goals originally intended by the reformers of the seventh century, the emperor, the court, and the aristocracy at the capital were able to survive, even prosper, for more than four centuries. They were able to do so largely because of the rise of private estates, called *shōen,* which gradually encroached on the public lands directly under the political and financial control of the imperial government. The private estates replaced official emoluments from the state as the principal source of aristocratic wealth, and permitted the court aristocrats to exercise more personal control over land and people in the provinces. They did so, however, not as public officials but as great private landholders whose interests were paradoxically antagonistic to the state they served as officials.

The adoption of a Chinese-style land and tax system had not excluded the idea of private holding of land. Even under the legal codes there were many exceptions to the principle that the emperor was "the master of all the land of the country." The new land

and tax system had applied only to rice land. Certain aristocratic families received outright grants of land, which they were entitled to hold for several generations and sometimes in perpetuity, without periodic redistribution. The imperial family also held many fields as a kind of private possession, and so too did the great Buddhist temples and Shinto shrines receiving the special patronage of the throne. By the middle of the eighth century, in order to encourage the reclamation of uncultivated land, the imperial government also granted more or less permanent land rights to those who opened new fields. Edicts issued in 743 and 772 provided that those who cleared new lands were entitled to full possession of them. Naturally, those who were already rich and powerful with large numbers of peasants at their disposal were in the best position to take advantage of these edicts. As a result, large agglomerations of rice land became the more or less permanent holdings of the imperial family, the leading aristocratic families, the large religious establishments at the capital, and certain local families that exploited the authority of provincial office for their own advantage.

These privately held lands became the nucleus of an extensive system of private estates free from periodic land redistribution and from imperial taxes. Certain high officials enjoyed temporary or permanent tax exemption on their lands, as did those who reclaimed new land, and all large landholders were anxious to enjoy this privilege. By the tenth century it had become the practice for landed proprietors to escape the burden of paying national dues to the government by securing charters that made their lands immune from the payment of the rice tax, the local produce tax, and the labor service tax. They frequently secured immunity from administrative interference by provincial officials as well. Local authorities were prohibited from entering the land of the tax-immune estate or from tampering with its administration. The granting of these immunities, though it was obviously of long-run disadvantage to the finances of the imperial government, was made possible by the cooperation of officials, both at the capital and in the provinces, who were no longer interested in rigorous enforcement of the law codes.

The imperial family presided over the creation of the estate system with only sporadic or intermittent protest. As taxable land began to disappear from the tax registers, reform-minded emperors occasionally attempted to stay the process by investigating estate charters or by reviving the old population census and land-distribution system. But their efforts were unsuccessful. Not only did the estate holders constitute a powerful vested interest at the capital, but there were obvious advantages to creating estates that would provide income for the imperial family itself. By the eleventh century, many emperors and their families had converted parts of the dwindling public domain into private proprietorships of their own. Indeed, by 1100 the imperial family was one of the chief estate proprietors within the country. Patches of public domain remained, but most cultivated areas were under private proprietorships.

Private estates grew in size and number by a snowball process. Sometimes estate holders would purchase neighboring fields and add them to their own lands, but more frequently the estates grew through the process of commendation. Local landholders, either peasants living on public land or small landholders who had reclaimed land for themselves, would place their fields in the hands of a more powerful, tax-immune landholder in order to escape the burden of public taxation. Usually commendation took the form of an outright grant of land in return for the right to use or cultivate the land in perpetuity on payment of a small rent. Commendation had economic advantages, but it also protected the commender from provincial or district officials who were often both corrupt and rapacious.

The Japanese estate was different from a twentieth-century one, and certainly different from the European manor. Its fields were not all in one place, it did not center on a manor house or seigneurial residence, and it had no seigneurial demesne farmed by the boon work of the peasantry. It was a group of plots, often scattered, that were bound together under a common proprietor. The proprietor, who might be the head of a powerful local family, a member of the aristocracy or the imperial family, or a religious institution, inherited the immunities created by the establishment of the estate and held most of the key powers over the land. If the proprietor did not feel himself influential enough to protect his rights against predatory officials, he would frequently seek out the patronage of a more powerful family or religious institution that would agree to guarantee the legality of the estate and to assure the continuation of its tax and administrative immunities. This patron, who usually had influence at the capital, was known as the "protector of the estate."

Many of the smaller estate proprietors, especially those who had reclaimed uncultivated areas, lived on the land itself. But many proprietors and estate protectors were absentee landholders who resided at the capital. They would appoint resident estate managers to superintend the cultivation of the land, collect rents, keep records, and settle problems that might arise among the peasants who tilled the soil. Frequently the estate managers were descended from the landholders who had commended their lands to the original proprietor of the estate. It was they who ran the affairs of the estate while the proprietors lived a life of leisure at the capital. Since the imperial government had begun to atrophy as a public institution, the private estate had become not only the main source of wealth for the aristocrats, but also the principal link between the capital and the provinces. For the peasants who worked the estate, the managers often provided the only effective local government.

The relations of the protector, the proprietor, the estate manager, and the peasant cultivator to the land were expressed in rights called *shiki*. Though originally this word meant "office," implying certain duties toward the land, it came to have the meaning of "profit from the land" or, more precisely, "a right to profit from the land." It might be best to think of a *shiki* as a kind of deed or title that specified its holder's claims to a portion of the harvest as well as his obligations to others in the hierarchy of rights to the estate. The *shiki* of the cultivator, for example, gave him the right to live on a particular plot of land and till it in return for the payment of an annual rent. The estate manager's *shiki* might entitle him to a share of the harvest in return for managing the peasantry and sending their rents to the proprietor. Generally speaking, the *shiki* of the estate proprietor was the closest to a clear right of land ownership as we understand it. It might not be the most profitable right over the land, but it was certainly the most inclusive. The proprietor had the power to survey the land, to keep land records, to alienate the land, and even to exercise police powers over its occupants.

The hierarchy of *shiki* was by no means a rigid one. *Shiki* could be bought, sold, inherited, and even divided. Though in origin the system was relatively simple, it soon grew enormously complicated. As the result of inheritance or sale over the course of several generations, a single individual might hold several kinds of *shiki* on one estate, or perhaps be a holder of *shiki* in several estates. The proprietor of one estate might hold a proprietor's *shiki* or even a manager's *shiki* in several others. Further down the hierarchy, a middling-size landholder might hold a manager's *shiki* on several fields, a cultivator's *shiki* on others, and perhaps even part of a proprietor's *shiki* on a neighboring estate. It would therefore be a mistake to view the estate as a neat unit of landholding under the complete control of a single landlord. Rather, it was primarily a legal device for permitting large numbers of people to share in the profit of the land in an age when land rather than money was the principal source of wealth.

*   *   *

At first glance, it seems difficult to find anything in the institutions of eleventh-century Japan that resemble those of northwestern Europe in the eighth or ninth centuries. The estate system was very dif-

ferent from the manorial system that had characterized land holding in Europe. The economic bases of
Japanese agriculture, with its highly productive rice
agriculture, probably made Japan a much wealthier
culture than Europe with its extensive rainfall agriculture. The aristocracy at Heian was far more elegant, far more sophisticated, and far more literate
than the half-barbarian courts of the Franks, Ger-
mans, and the Anglo-Saxons; and doubtless the Japanese courtiers would have regarded the European aristocracy as crude and boorish. And finally, while the
institutions of the Roman state existed as a patch-
work of half-forgotten practices, partly absorbed by
the rude monarchies of Europe and partly taken over
by the church, the imperial institution and the elaborate structure of government offices inspired by
T'ang China remained intact in Japan. Yet in certain
important respects, the two cultures resembled one
another: the effectiveness of centralized authority had
undergone considerable decay, and the keeping of
local order was gradually shifting into the hands of
local fighting men. It was these two conditions that
led to the gradual emergence of a feudal style of government.

Chapter 3

From
Civil Monarchy to
Warrior
Rule

The fusion of the Chinese idea of the state with traditional Japanese forms of social organization, like
the mixture of Roman ideas of sovereignty with Ger-
manic customs, produced a cultural milieu in which
feudal practices could flourish. But, as in Europe, the
more immediate stimulus to the emergence of a feudal political system in Japan was the need to preserve
local order where the centralized machinery of state
ceased to provide effective security for life and property. In Europe the delegation of public authority to
private individuals began under the Merovingian and
Carolingian rulers, who were as little able to make
a bureaucratic monarchy work as was the imperial
government of eleventh-century Japan. This trend
toward fragmentation of political power proceeded
at an accelerated pace under the impact of an outside
menace, the Viking raids from the north and west
coasts of Europe and the Magyar invasions from the
east. It was this military threat from a new wave of
barbarians that plunged Western Europe into feudalism. Since it was not possible to rely on the protection
of royal armies, local order was most easily preserved
by the creation of local bands for self-defense. Warriors looked for chiefs, and lords looked for vassals.
The insecurity created by the invasions accelerated

the spread of vassalage and the decay of central authority.

In Japan, however, the transition was less abrupt. Disorder was primarily internal in origin. The continued presence of unassimilated "barbarian" tribes on the northwestern frontier in Honshu, the prevalence of banditry and outlawry, and the outbreak of disputes over land rights were the principal sources of local turmoil. Japan never faced the same urgent threat of outside invasion. Given the relatively greater durability of the court, the emergence of full-fledged feudal decentralization was preceded by an attempt to bring feudal practices to the support of the moribund imperial government.

THE LOCAL WARRIOR

The imperial government early abandoned the elaborate system of conscription and local garrisons adopted from China. Military service was extremely burdensome to the average peasant family: sending a son to military service meant not only the loss of a working hand, but also added expense, because the conscript had to provide his own provisions and weapons. "If one man is conscripted," went a popular saying, "then one household will be ruined." Evasion of conscription was common, and often those peasants who were recruited did not make able fighting men. Since there was little or no need for a standing army, the government decided to modify the conscription system. By the end of the eighth century, local garrison units had ceased to exist except in frontier areas where so-called barbarian tribes fought the advance of Japanese settlers. Most of these border garrisons were recruited from the sons of local landed families, but throughout most of the country there was no permanent public instrument for the maintenance of local order. The provincial governor would sometimes have a private guard of kinsmen or retainers of local origin, but when a major military crisis threatened the imperial government, it had to rely on temporary levies of the local warrior class to enforce its authority in the provinces. Thus, the maintenance of local order gradually fell into the hands of this class.

These local warriors were not a new class, but one with roots of great antiquity. They were the social, if not biological, heirs of the old clan leaders. Indeed, a clan chieftain of the sixth century would probably have been far less startled by the sight of a warrior of the tenth century than he would have been by the painted aristocrats at the capital. Although the era of reform had brought about great change in political ideas and institutions and in the style of life at the capital, the provinces had been little affected.

The local warrior was set apart from the mass of the peasantry in the provinces by his status as a land-holder. Invariably he was either a small estate proprietor or an estate manager or official. It is not always clear how his land was originally acquired, but most historians believe that the local warrior-land-holders sprang either from a small landholding class created when the new land-distribution system was introduced in the seventh century or from families who had taken advantage of the land-reclamation edicts of the eighth century. With the growth of the estate system, many of these landholders became part of the new structure of land rights, retaining their freedom from land distribution and from the fiscal and administrative supervision of the provincial government. Those who were not strong enough or confident enough to remain independent proprietors commended their lands to court aristocrats or to more powerful neighbors.

Unlike those at the top of the estate system, however, the local warrior-landholders were settled on or near the lands over which they had rights. In the rich Kantō plain in central Honshu (see map), where the warrior class flourished most markedly, the typical warrior had deep roots in the countryside. He lived in a small compound protected by an earthen wall or wooden palisade and usually surrounded by a shallow ditch. The compound was not only used as his residence, but served as his administrative headquarters in normal times and could be converted into a small fort in time of disorder. Within the compound were dwellings for his family and his immediate followers, a storehouse for harvested rice and other valuables, and an armory for his weapons. Scattered about the landscape nearby were the rude huts of the peasants, who took part of their crops to the compound as annual rent at harvest time. Though the size of the warrior's holdings and the nature of his rights over the land varied widely from region to region, in most areas the compound and its surrounding peasant community formed the basic unit of local society.

The warrior's reliance on the labor of others for his livelihood lay at the base of his power. Because he did not have to cultivate his land, he could devote much of his time to honing his military skills. While the peasants worked the fields, the warrior could maintain his fighting prowess by hunting wild game from horseback in the hills and meadows near his land. If game were scarce, he could practice archery near the compound, shooting at a board or bamboo target from his galloping mount, or, if he wanted to improve his aim, at running dogs. The warrior had to be in constant readiness for attack, and so too did the other adult males in his family and the followers he kept about him.

Since land went hand in hand with local influence, and since influence with local government authorities was frequently necessary to protect one's land, the warriors were often intimately involved with the local government machinery. Sometimes they obtained posts as district officers responsible for collecting taxes on national land that remained outside the estate system; sometimes they held one of the many subordinate posts in the provincial government headquarters. In hopes of perpetuating their family's influence, local warriors often managed to have their official posts recognized as hereditary. Thus many posts in the local hierarchy were converted into their patrimony just as the offices in the central government had become the patrimony of the aristocracy. The difference was, of course, that although official positions in the capital were usually sinecures, those in the local hierarchy of government continued to be functional

—to exercise direct control over the collection of national taxes and the protection of local rights on the land.

The combination of land rights, military skill, and access to official position was a potent one. Although it would perhaps be a mistake to think of the warriors as a local aristocracy, they did constitute a local elite. More important, they were the only group in the provinces capable of creating or suppressing local rebellion, brigandage, or armed disputes. In times of trouble, which usually meant local trouble, the warriors formed themselves into bands or parties. In some ways these warrior bands resembled the sixth-century clans. They centered on a warrior family and were led by a family chief, who had certain ceremonial duties as well as military ones. The band might include not only the family chief's sons and brothers, but members of related or branch families as well. This is not surprising, since in time of trouble it was only natural to turn to one's kinsmen for help. But the warrior bands had other members, usually followers or retainers of the chief who lived in the compound of the family chief or his relatives. Unlike the clan, then, the warrior band was composed of both kin and unrelated members.

The dual character of the basic warrior band was reflected in the terms used to describe its members. Those most closely related to the chief of the band were called "sons of the house" (*ie no ko*); others who were called "housemen" (*kenin*), although not related by blood, were treated as family members; and finally some, whose status seems to have been relatively lower, were called "retainers" (*rōtō*) and were obligated to follow their chief in time of war and perhaps serve him in daily life in time of peace. Aside from members of the band, who were usually mounted fighting men, there were also unmounted squires or grooms, called "underlings" (*genin*) or simply "followers" (*shoju*). These men, really menial servants, were usually peasants who worked on the warrior's landholdings or on the estate of which he was a manager. They did not engage in fighting at the time of battle, but they did perform other essential functions. Even a small warrior band, consisting perhaps of a chief, his brother or son, and one or two retainers, needed seven or eight servants to tend their horses, forage for food and supplies, and wait on their masters' other wants.

The bonds that held the family-centered warrior band together were those of personal loyalty as well as of blood. There are few documents that let us glimpse the nature of these ties, but early war tales such as the *Tale of Mutsu* (*Mutsu waki*) and the *Tale of Masakado* (*Shōmonki*) suggest that they were not very different from early forms of vassalage in Europe. There was no formal ceremony whereby one individual made himself the "man" of another, but it is clear that the same kind of dependent relationship was involved. The tie between the leader of a warrior band and his followers was a warm one, expected to last the lifetime of both. If need be, the follower was to give his life freely in the service of his leader, and often deliberately followed him in death when he was killed in battle. Ideally a warrior did not have two masters, and a renegade who turned on his leader was regarded as the most contemptible of men. The follower's loyal service was often repaid with some material reward. The chief of a warrior band might support some of his retainers in his household, and after a battle would bestow on his followers booty or lands confiscated from the enemy. The follower did not ask his leader for favors, for the loyalty he gave was regarded as a natural duty that was its own reward.

Whatever the position of the individual warrior in the band and whatever his relation to his leader, he placed a high value on the ideal of personal bravery and had nothing but contempt for those who showed cowardice. In the code of the warrior, a warrior should never turn his back on the enemy or attempt escape. Even when he was outnumbered and defeat was certain, it was better to fight to the end. The early war tales abound with stories of valiant warriors who plunge into the ranks of the enemy, determined to perish in the saddle rather than face the shame of capture or retreat. To die with the sense of having fought valorously was far preferable than living with the knowledge of having been vanquished by fear. In part this outlook reflected a fatalistic view of life. Death was the natural fate of "those who wield the bow and arrow," and the warrior could not escape its inexorable advance. But equally important was the warrior's desire to avoid dishonor to his name. Warriors were imbued with a great pride of birth. A warrior was expected not only to fulfill his obligations to his chief, but also to enhance the glory of his family. Often before plunging into combat, a warrior would shout his name, his ancestry, the military exploits of his family, and his own prowess. This practice, known as "reading the family roll," is often described with great drama in the war tales.

Warriors fought with gusto, steeped in an admiration for physical strength and a delight in violence. Early military romances rarely depict the carnage and destruction of battle, nor do they describe the bloodiness, confusion, and terror which at least a few of its participants must have felt. Rather, they celebrate fighting as a glorious and ennobling enterprise that gives men a chance to demonstrate their boldness, daring, and gallantry. Their heroes are strong and fearless men, larger than life, who fight with exuberance, sublime confidence in their prowess, and scant regard for death. The *Tale of Mutsu,** for example, describes Minamoto Yoshiie (1041–1108), a historical figure later apotheosized as a paragon of military virtue, in the following breathless passage:

He shot arrows from horseback like a god; undeterred by gleaming blades, he lunged through the enemy's encirclements to emerge on their left and right. With his great arrowheads he transfixed one enemy chieftain after another, never shooting at random, but always inflicting a mortal wound. He galloped like the wind and fought

---

* Helen Craig McCullough (tr.), "A Tale of Mutsu," *Harvard Journal of Asiatic Studies,* Vol. XXV (1964–1965), pp. 178–211.

with a skill that was more than human. The barbarians fled rather than face him. . . .

Although the ordinary warrior could not achieve such superhuman feats in real life, the portrait of such a model fighting man gave him an ideal. Moreover, though the passage doubtless magnifies Yoshiie's deeds, it gives us some notion of the qualities a warrior leader needed to command the respect of his followers. One can well imagine that for such a man the warrior would gladly die.

This high regard for physical strength, individual gallantry, and even for recklessness was well suited to the warriors' style of combat. Since warrior bands were made up of mounted horsemen, fighting tended to be man to man. Battles were less the clash of massed armies, carefully grouped and maneuvered by their leaders, than a series of fights between individual combatants. To be sure, battles often began with a certain degree of formality. Opposing forces exchanged emissaries to agree on a time and location for battle, and once they had drawn themselves up in readiness, they would each send forth a representative to proclaim the justice of their own cause and the villainy of their enemies. But once this "battle of the vocal chords" was ended and the two forces had exchanged several volleys of arrows, their formations would break and the battle would become a general melee. Individual warriors would ride into the ranks of the enemy, shooting and slashing as they went. Frequently, a warrior would pair off with one of the enemy to engage in single combat, hoping to unhorse his opponent and finish him off with a sword blow. If he were outnumbered or in need of rescue, his kinsmen and followers would often join in to help him out. This type of combat was not only undisciplined—it was not particularly lethal. To inflict a fatal blow in the midst of such confusion was difficult, and most casualties probably resulted from arrow wounds.

The outcome of the battle became clear only when the forces of one side turned in rout, perhaps in the hope of preserving their strength for future clashes, and the leader of the winning side gave a shout of victory. After the battle came the granting of honors, the dividing of booty, and the giving of rewards. The greatest prize was to have taken the head of a well-known enemy leader. Usually the victorious leader would hold an inspection of heads taken to make sure that they did not include those of his comrades or artificial heads contrived by followers hungry for reward. It was also a great honor to have struck the first blow against the enemy, and such a display of boldness was the occasion for special honor. Given the confused nature of the fighting, warriors usually had to have a witness to their deeds. They therefore frequently wore some sort of insignia so they could be easily identified later: The armor of a particular warrior was bound by cords or braid of a distinctive color, and a small banner with the crest or name of the family was attached to his helmet.

THE
POLITICAL
EMERGENCE
OF THE
WARRIOR
CHIEFTAINS

The family-centered warrior bands were effective in settling local disputes over land and protecting the local community against brigands and bandits, but they were hardly sufficient to deal with a military crisis of larger dimension. By the late tenth and early eleventh centuries, such crises began to occur with frequency. Beginning with the rebellions of Taira Masakado and Fujiwara Sumitomo in 935, certain powerful warrior chieftains in the provinces took advantage of the military weakness of the imperial government to defy its authority and challenge the power of its local representatives. In 1028 came the revolt of Taira Tadatsune, and during the late eleventh century the defiance of the powerful Kiyowara and Abe families in northeastern Honshu.

In order to crush the risings of such rebel warrior chieftains and disturbances of a similar nature, the imperial government was forced to rely on the services of other provincial warrior leaders who could rally an army made up of local warrior bands. In the case of serious revolts, the court would issue a temporary commission to a local warrior leader to raise forces, pursue and arrest the rebels, and punish them. Usually the recipients of these commissions were not ordinary warriors but men set apart by the extent of their landholdings or by illustrious family origins. Often they were descendants of younger sons or cadet branches of the imperial family or of aristocratic families who had come to the provinces as officials and then stayed on the land rather than return to the capital, where the future held little for them. Their distinguished origins made them natural candidates to lead regional alliances of warriors against the enemies of the court. Though appointed only for the duration of the emergency, the recipients of such imperial commissions often held them indefinitely.

These regional alliances were of a more temporary character than the small family-centered warrior band, but they did enhance the reputation of the families who led them. The leaders of these families were known as "warrior chieftains" (*bushi no tōryō*). Although most of the warriors who joined in a regional alliance during times of crisis went their separate ways after it had subsided, these alliances sometimes became the basis of more permanent ties. Allegiance to a warrior chieftain or his descendants became a matter of pride for some lesser leaders, and often this loyalty passed from generation to generation. In any case, it was natural that in the face of the growing insecurity produced by the military weakness of the throne, local warrior families should rally to chieftains who could offer them physical protection. Such protection had become far more important than the legal protection afforded by the estate protectors living far off at the capital.

The emergence of warrior chieftains able to rally large regional alliances of small warrior bands in the provinces at first constituted little threat to the imperial government and the aristocracy at the capital. Although the aristocrats regarded the warriors as their social inferiors, referring to the fighting men of the Kantō region as the "eastern barbarians," they found them useful not only in crushing local disturbances or rebellions, but also in keeping order at

Taira had originally settled in the Kantō region, and one of their members had won the favor of the court by suppressing the rebellion of Taira Masakado. The leaders of the Seiwa branch of the Minamoto had also made their reputation in the service of the court by suppressing the revolt of Taira Tadatsune, and later in the long series of campaigns against the Abe and Kiyowara families in the northeast. By the late eleventh century, as the prestige of the Seiwa branch of the Minamoto grew among the warriors of the east, the Ise Taira put down stronger roots in the west of Japan. They began to acquire land rights and influence in the regions closer to the capital, especially near the imperial shrine at Ise and along the Inland Sea. Just as the Minamoto had established themselves as the "claws of the Fujiwara" in the eleventh century, the Ise Taira managed to ingratiate themselves with the imperial court through the suppression of piracy along the Inland Sea. By the mid-twelfth century, both great warrior lines had important connections at the capital, which they guarded jealously.

The rising importance of the great warrior chieftains who led the Minamoto and Taira should not be thought of as the beginnings of a class struggle between the warriors and the aristocracy. The leaders of the Taira and the Minamoto regarded themselves as aristocratic in origin, took great pains to establish their pedigrees, and intermarried with aristocratic families. They accepted aristocratic standards of prestige and saw themselves as deputies of imperial authority. Yet there were temptations for the warrior chieftains to use their influence at court to extend their personal power, precisely because they regarded themselves as noble in origin. Certain of the great aristocratic families, such as the Fujiwara, had already shown how it was possible to secure great advantage for one's family by marrying into the imperial family, and what the Fujiwara had done with nubile daughters and astute political sense could be accomplished all the more easily by chieftains who commanded large bands of warriors.

In the latter half of the twelfth century, the bal-

the capital. The rough-and-ready fighting me
the eastern provinces made good bodyguard
they were often employed in armed retinues fo
tocratic families, as guards at the imperial p
and as members of the capital police force. In
the term *samurai,** which many Western histo
generally use to mean warrior, originally meant a
son who served the emperor, the crown princes
certain high officials in the government. The n
for the services of the warriors grew particula
acute in the late eleventh and early twelfth centur
as lawlessness spread to the capital and its environ
Banditry, robbery, and arson at the mansions o
wealthy aristocrats were common. Equally important
the great Buddhist monasteries on the outskirts o
the city maintained large armies of monks w
fought with those of rival sects or temples. Of
these clashes would spill over into the capital its
adding to the uncertainty and disorder of life th

The court and the aristocracy relied on the s
ices of two families of regional warrior chieftain
particular, the Seiwa branch of the Minamoto fa
and the Ise branch of the Taira family. Both w
descendants of early ninth-century emperors wh
had given aristocratic surnames to their children
offspring and provided them with lucrative posts a
the capital or in the provinces.† The Ise branch of th

---

* The word *samurai* derives from the verb *saburau*, "to wai
upon or serve a lord or sovereign." At first only warriors wh
had followers or retainers were referred to as samurai. It wa
not until the seventeenth and eighteenth centuries that the
term became synonymous with "warrior" in common usage.
The more general term applied to members of the warrior class
throughout premodern Japanese history was *bushi*, which meant
simply a person whose main occupation was the military arts.
† This curious practice requires some explanation. Descendants o
an emperor not in the direct line of succession lost their statu
as members of the imperial family after a fixed number of ge
erations. Given the polygamous marriage customs of the cou
emperors were often quite prolific and produced dozens of
scendants who had to be provided for. Since the imperial fa
had no surname, surnames were granted to give them a
status, and official posts were provided to set them on their
economically.

ance of power among the Minamoto and Taira chieftains, the court aristocracy, and the imperial government began to undergo serious alteration. As a result of intrigues among the aristocracy, the warrior chieftains were drawn into the politics of the capital and proved themselves able to exercise a decisive influence. In 1156, for example, two aristocratic factions at Kyoto struggled for control over succession to the throne. The leaders of both factions called on one or the other of the Taira and Minamoto chieftains for support. Each of the warrior chieftains at the court, anxious to destroy the influence of his rivals at the capital, mobilized his followers for battle. The struggle cut across family lines. The son of the Minamoto family leader made joint cause with the Taira, and certain Taira chieftains allied themselves with the Minamoto. Victory went to Taira Kiyomori (1118–1181), the leader of the Ise Taira. He also proved successful in 1159 when his former ally Minamoto Yoshitomo (1123–1160) attempted to drive him from his position. With the power of the Minamoto swept from the capital, Kiyomori had paramount influence over the court.

Using his position as champion of the winning court faction and backed by the implicit threat of his military power, Kiyomori began to have his relatives and allies appointed to important posts in provincial governments and to extend the land rights of his warrior followers over both the public domain and the private estates. Borrowing a practice established by the Fujiwara, he managed to marry one of his daughters into the imperial family, and in 1180 his infant grandson, the offspring of this marriage, ascended the throne. The supremacy of the Taira proved to be only temporary, however, for Kiyomori's influence outside the capital was weak. He was more the leader of an aristocratic clique than the leader of a regional warrior alliance, and he had done little to extend his power over the rest of the warrior class. He had succeeded in dominating the politics of the court, but he had by no means established the kind of local order that was needed so acutely in the provinces, nor had he strengthened his position in the key Kantō region. This ultimately proved the undoing of the Taira leadership, for it left them without an adequate base of support.

The collapse of Taira ascendancy came during the Gempei War of 1180–1185, a five-year struggle between the entrenched Taira and the resurgent leadership of the Minamoto. The war began when Minamoto Yoritomo (1147–1199), the exiled son of Yoshitomo, allied with certain aristocratic malcontents at the capital to raise the banner of revolt against the alleged tyranny of Kiyomori. Yoritomo, who had been raised in Izu on the edge of the Kantō region, possessed an astute sense of the needs and psychology of the warrior class. Exploiting their desire for land and security, he rallied the support of many local warrior families in central Honshu. He was also aided by the wise and dashing generalship of his uncle and his brother, who won a series of victories against Taira allies in the early stages of the war. Confronted by this combination of Minamoto political and military success, the Taira were driven from the capital, and in 1185 their armies were finally defeated in the west. The victory left Yoritomo the most powerful warrior chieftain in the country, and, building on his position, he established a far more durable ascendancy than Kiyomori had.

THE
ESTABLISHMENT
OF THE
KAMAKURA
BAKUFU

The victory of the Minamoto forces marked an important turning point in Japanese history, for it resulted in the establishment of the Kamakura *bakufu* or "tent government," a more or less centralized political regime that rested solidly on the customs and institutions of the warrior class. The bakufu was not intended to destroy the imperial government or even to supplant it. On the contrary, Yoritomo saw himself as a defender of the throne and the rights of the aristocracy: he had no idea of challenging imperial authority. The bakufu grew out of the exigencies of the Gempei War. Yoritomo had established his headquarters at Kamakura, a small fishing village on the edge of the strategic Kantō region, where he could maintain a firm grip on the local warriors and chieftains who followed him in the fight against the Taira. Once the war was over, however, the administrative practices he employed to lead his followers became institutionalized in a permanent political structure. These institutions persisted partly because of Yoritomo's desire to perpetuate his own ascendancy, but mainly because they provided a measure of the local order and security that the imperial bureaucracy had failed to maintain.

Yoritomo attempted to rule by relying heavily on the ties of vassalage that bound the warrior class. The great warrior alliance he built up in the early stages of the Gempei War was very much like the family-centered warrior band or the earlier regional alliances of warriors, except that it was national in scale. After 1185 this warrior alliance became the core of a "government by vassalage." Those warriors who rallied to the Minamoto, whether they had been followers of the family for generations or whether they were won over only after the outbreak of fighting with the Taira, became the personal vassals of Yoritomo. They were known as *gokenin* or "honorable housemen," the honorific prefix *go-* distinguishing them from the housemen (*kenin*) of ordinary warrior leaders. Yoritomo was personally acquainted with many of his vassals, whose strengths and weaknesses of character he knew intimately and whose loyalty he demanded with fierce jealousy. A considerable number of the *gokenin* had audiences with Yoritomo at which they pledged their fidelity, in much the same way that vassals performed homage in early European feudalism. This relationship was not contractual, for it rested on no legal document and could not be created, altered, or abrogated by any legal process. Rather, it was a one-sided pledge of support, loyalty, and service to Yoritomo, whose effective power was greater than that of the court or the aristocracy and to whom they therefore looked for leadership and protection.

Although the allegiance of Yoritomo's vassals rested both on his military strength and on intense personal feeling, the bond was often cemented by material rewards. Like the local warrior leader who divided booty among his followers, Yoritomo gave his vassals grants of *shiki,* or land rights. For those who had long-standing rights over a certain estate or part of an estate, he would give a grant of confirmation. This was a firmer guarantee than could be provided by the increasingly feeble protectors of the estates living at the capital. Yoritomo would also frequently grant *shiki* to new lands, sometimes from estates controlled by the Minamoto family itself, but more often from lands or estates confiscated from the Taira and their followers. The grant of new land rights was usually given in perpetuity. The confirmation or granting of land rights—guaranteed by the military strength of Yoritomo—was conceived of largely as a reward for the follower's service during the war. In return for these rewards, Yoritomo expected a complete, unconditional, and open-ended commitment of loyalty from the *gokenin.* All his vassals, regardless of how much or how little they received, were expected to serve "with a uniform spirit of devotion and at any moment . . . be prepared to lay down their lives in repayment for the favors received." In normal times, they were expected to provide guard service at the bakufu headquarters in Kamakura or at the court in Kyoto; in time of war, they were expected to rally to arms at the summons of the bakufu. The duties of the *gokenin* were therefore much less specific than those of the vassal in Europe, whose obligations were usually spelled out more concretely.

The creation of the *gokenin* provided Yoritomo with a body of men to whom he entrusted extensive powers of local government. The more powerful of his vassals were given the post of provincial constable (*shugo*). These officials were initially appointed in every province that came under Yoritomo's control to work side by side with the provincial governor appointed from the capital. After 1190 they were established in every province in the country. The duties of the provincial constables were public ones, intended to provide the kind of local security the imperial government had not been able to maintain. They were charged with the chastising of local rebels, the pursuit and apprehension of murderers, and the raising of military forces from the *gokenin* of the province for guard duty or in time of trouble. The appointment of the provincial constables was extremely important, for the post gave its holder not only considerable powers over the direct vassals of Kamakura who lived within the province, but also police powers over the general populace. Because such a combination of powers was potentially very influential, Yoritomo (and his successors) attempted to check the provincial constables by preventing men from serving as constables in their native provinces and by exercising the right to dismiss the constables at will.

At the same time, Yoritomo appointed many of his vassals as land stewards (*jitō*) on private estates throughout the country. The ostensible purpose of this office was to protect the proprietary rights of absentee landholders—particularly those of the court aristocracy, the imperial family, and the great religious institutions, many of whom had suffered expropriation under the Taira or during the wars of the 1180s. The function of the land steward was first of all to ensure the collection of rents on the estate and to see that the estate proprietor or protector received his proper share. But he also possessed certain functions of the old estate managers. He could, for example, maintain peace and order on the estate, see to it that criminals were properly punished, settle disputes among the resident cultivators on the estate, and supervise the management of the land itself. But perhaps the most important thing was that the appointment of land stewards provided Yoritomo with a means of rewarding followers to whom he could not grant new land rights. Appointment as a land steward took the form of a grant of a *shiki*, which, of course, provided the holder with income. Usually the stewards were appointed from among the less powerful of Yoritomo's vassals. Many of these men already held the position of manager on the estate to which they were appointed steward, but many of them were established on the land by this new office. To be sure, at first not every estate in the country had a land steward appointed by Yoritomo, particularly since the western provinces were under only very loose control by Kamakura; but by the 1190s Yoritomo was appointing them in ever-increasing numbers.

The new "government by vassalage," spawned on the battlefield, needed legal justification. In 1185, with the defeat of the Taira and the establishment of Yoritomo's military supremacy, the imperial government was persuaded to grant Yoritomo the right to appoint constables and land stewards and to recognize him as both Constable-General and Steward-General of the whole country. Although the court had little choice in the matter, the new arrangements, particularly the appointment of land stewards, served the interests of the court and the aristocracy as much as it served those of Yoritomo and the warrior class. The final legitimization of the new regime came in 1192, when the emperor appointed Yoritomo as *shōgun*, or *Sei-i-tai-shōgun* (literally, "Barbarian-suppressing General"). This title had originally been granted to warrior chieftains or imperial generals commissioned to fight the "barbarians" in the northeast. It implied the authority of Yoritomo to preserve the national peace, just as it had earlier given the leaders of regional warrior alliances temporary powers to preserve local order. Eventually, however, the office of shogun became that of a warrior monarch whose authority was derived from the imperial government but whose effective power eclipsed it.

THE
CONSOLIDATION
OF THE
BAKUFU

While Yoritomo remained alive, the Kamakura bakufu was a highly personal instrument and remained under his autocratic control. With his death in 1199, however, the bakufu faced a crisis of leadership. Although Yoritomo was an astute leader of men and a gifted administrative innovator, he was not very successful as a dynast. Partly by chance and partly as a result of Yoritomo's distrust of his own immediate kin, the Minamoto family was not able to retain the office of shogun. The other Minamoto leaders who had won military victories in the Gempei War had either died in battle or had been removed as political rivals by Yoritomo's deliberate design. His own offspring proved ill suited to shouldering the responsibilities of personal rule, and by the early thirteenth century control over the government at Kamakura fell into the hands of the more important vassals. From 1205 until the fall of the bakufu in 1334 administrative supervision and policy decisions were placed in the hands of shogunal regents appointed from the powerful Hōjō family, who governed in the name of the shogun with the aid of a council of the most powerful vassals. The shogun became a mere puppet, and was no longer a member of the Minamoto clan. After 1226 the post was held by a series of aristocrats and imperial princes.

Despite the change in the personal leadership of the bakufu, it continued to maintain control over the warrior class. The tie established between Yoritomo and the original band of vassals persisted through their heirs. When the original *gokenin* pledged loyalty to Yoritomo, they spoke not only for themselves but for their whole family, including their immediate kinsmen and branch families as well. The obligation to serve the "lord of Kamakura" passed from the head of a *gokenin* family to his successor, and it was through this hereditary transmission of loyalty that the bakufu maintained the support of its vassals. This gave the Kamakura regime a much broader base than it might first appear to have had, for it was through the heads of *gokenin* families that the bakufu dealt with much of the warrior class. Orders for guard service at the capital and at Kamakura or for military service in time of war were issued through the constables to the heads of vassal families. It was also to the family heads that the bakufu sent requests for special financial levies, which were borne not only by them as the direct vassals of the bakufu but also apportioned among their followers. The bakufu did all it could to strengthen the position of the family head, for it was he who served as the main agent for the transmission of the bakufu's orders to the bulk of the warrior class.

As "government by vassalage" became hereditary, it gradually began to supplant the imperial government as the only effective government in most parts of the country. Although the power of the bakufu continued to be cloaked in the mantle of imperial legitimacy and although the bakufu continued to insist that it would not encroach upon the jurisdiction of older established institutions—whether the imperial government, the estate proprietors, or the great religious sects—its writ inevitably became more powerful. In part this was a matter of attrition. With the appointment of provincial constables and land stewards, the old machinery of provincial government ceased to have any real meaning, and during the course of the thirteenth century the imperially appointed provincial governments seem to have fallen into disuse. Some functions of the provincial governors, such as the repair of temples and shrines and the upkeep of roads, by default gravitated into the hands of the constable.

Perhaps more striking was the penetration of Kamakura's power into the court itself. After the establishment of the bakufu, relations between Kyoto and Kamakura, although correct, had never been cordial. In 1221 Go-Toba, an abdicated emperor, prompted by resentment at the military upstarts in the east, organized a revolt against the bakufu, drawing support from certain aristocratic families, monasteries, and small warrior families in the capital region. Prompt action by the bakufu suppressed the revolt, known as the Shōkyū War, and the victory enabled the Kamakura regime to consolidate its position in the west, where its power had been weak. Over 3,000 estates belonging to the rebellious nobles and monasteries were confiscated. In some cases the bakufu granted its vassals proprietary rights on the confiscated domains, and in others it appointed them as land stewards with financial advantages nearly as

profitable as those of the proprietors. Equally important, the uprising provided the Kamakura regime
with an excuse to place its representative directly in
the capital to guard against the renewal of plots
against the bakufu. Not only did these representatives supervise the selection of aristocrats to all high
posts in the court, but they also kept watch on the
abdication and succession of emperors. There was little question as to whether Kamakura or Kyoto really
ruled Japan.

The suppression of the Shōkyū rebels ushered in a
half-century of relative peace and stability. Symbolic
of the final consolidation of bakufu power was the
issuance of a new legal code, the Jōei Formulary, in
1232. Although it did not supplant the old Chinese-
style codes, it provided a body of law more closely
attuned to the needs and practices of the warrior
class. Drafted to give systematic form to the legal
and administrative customs followed by the bakufu
in its early days, it gave clear definition to the duties
of constables and land stewards; regulated the title,
succession, and assignment of land tenure rights; defined certain major crimes and their punishments;
and established regular judicial procedures for the
settlement of disputes over land and the administration of criminal justice. The new code marked the
growing tendency for practices of the warrior class
to become the basis of law as well as government. Indeed, its precepts became a guide for feudal law-
makers in later centuries. Of more immediate importance, however, the new code provided such a
prompt and regular system for the resolution of disputes among the *gokenin* that many other warriors
and even many aristocrats brought their suits to the
courts at Kamakura. Because the courts were kept
under close supervision to ensure that all suits were
given a fair hearing and because the bakufu peri-
odically inspected the affairs of the constables and
land stewards, the Kamakura government was able to
provide fair and impartial redress of grievances and
abuses until its dissolution in the late thirteenth century. Indeed, its capacity to settle disputes over land

by law rather than by force probably enabled it to survive as long as it did.

*　　*　　*

In many ways the Kamakura bakufu resembled the Carolingian empire. Both regimes were final way stations on the path toward a purely feudal political order. In form the Kamakura bakufu, like the Carolingian empire, attempted to vest itself in the raiments of an older tradition of public authority. Just as Charlemagne turned to Rome, so Yoritomo turned to Kyoto to acquire legitimization and moral sanction for his power. But in practice neither leader expected to bring about the revival of a bureaucratic state. In consolidating or buttressing their political power, both men relied heavily on the ties of vassalage, cemented with grants of land or official position, to secure the loyalty of their powerful subjects. In spirit "government by vassalage" under the Kamakura shogunate was much like what some historians have called "Carolingian feudalism." It could be said of Yoritomo, as it has been said of Charlemagne, that his vassals became his officials and his officials became his vassals. The *gokenin* might well be compared to the *vassi dominici* of ninth-century France, and the provincial constables to the Frankish counts. In both Kamakura Japan and Carolingian France the extension of vassalage ties between a warrior monarch and local warrior chieftains, and the incorporation of these ties into the framework of government institutions, represented a compromise between the dying tradition of centralized rule and the existence of an aggressive provincial warrior class. In Japan after 1300, as in France after 900, the compromise broke down and the warrior class gradually liquidated the last vestiges of centralized political organization.

Chapter 4

From Warrior Rule to Feudal Anarchy

It is no easier to assign a specific date for the onset of full feudalism in Japan than it is for Europe. By 1300 a horse-riding warrior class dominated the countryside, the system of vassalage was widely practiced, and warrior leaders at the highest level of society made grants of land or office to their followers as a reward for loyal service. But the full devolution of public power into the hands of local feudal lords had not yet been completed. Although the imperial government had declined to the point of complete ineffectiveness by the middle of the thirteenth century, the estate system and the bakufu still served to bind the provinces to some form of central control. It took nearly two centuries for these last remnants of central authority to be sloughed off by the aggressive and land-hungry local warrior class. Not surprisingly, the process was accompanied by the onset of incessant local warfare in the early fourteenth century.

The primary motor behind this warfare was the intense land hunger of the local warriors, who were under many pressures to increase their holdings. Usually warrior families were large, and the family head needed new land to provide for his numerous offspring. Equally important, the practice of equal inheritance also stimulated the desire to enlarge family holdings. When a warrior died, his property was shared by all his sons rather than bequeathed to one of them. As a result, landholdings were broken into smaller and smaller portions with each generation, and often these parcels were too small to maintain their holders in warrior status. Primogeniture or indivisible inheritance was slow in developing, and local warriors looked for other means to aggrandize their landholdings. The easiest method was to expropriate land from the estate proprietors at Kyoto who could not defend themselves militarily. The lands of the warrior's neighbors, or even those of his personal lord, were equally tempting prizes. The warrior class therefore welcomed warfare not merely as a chance to establish one's fame and glory for posterity, but as an opportunity to encroach on the land rights of others.

By the late fifteenth century chronic local warfare resulted in the emergence of local feudal lords who used the practice of vassalage and the granting of fiefs to piece together small consolidated domains similar to the baronies of twelfth- and thirteenth-century Europe. The countryside was scattered with castles and fortifications that, like those of European feudal lords, served as capital, military headquarters, and court for the localities surrounding them. The local feudal lord exercised public powers as a matter of private prerogative. If his right to exercise these powers was challenged, the challenge came not from above but from neighboring lords or rebellious vassals. Local disorder was constant and political fragmentation complete. By 1500 feudal government in Japan had reached the same stage of development as it had in Europe four centuries earlier.

THE DECLINE
OF BAKUFU
AUTHORITY

The decline of the bakufu was central to the onset of full political feudalism. Although Yoritomo's system had succeeded in providing more or less centralized government for a century, the discipline it exercised over its vassals and the rest of the warrior class was clearly disintegrating by the end of the thirteenth century. In part the breakdown of the Kamakura regime was due to faltering leadership. By the early 1300s, corruption had begun to erode the bakufu. The Hōjō family, who as regents had dominated the administration of the bakufu for nearly a century, and their vassals began to place their own interests above those of public order. Bakufu courts no longer dispensed impartial justice, and high officials were often incompetent. The shogunal regents, selected from the young and immature members of the Hōjō family, were unable to provide viable leadership and were often under the influence of unscrupulous favorites. A particularly bad example was Hōjō Takatoki (1303–1333). According to the *Taiheiki*, a military romance chronicling the downfall of the bakufu, his fondness for dogs was so great that he kept several thousand of them at Kamakura, fattened with delicacies and bedecked with gold and silver jewelry. The quality of the administration could hardly have inspired much confidence under these circumstances.

Probably more important than these personal factors in the breakdown of "government by vassalage" was the decay of the vassalage tie itself. With the passage of several generations, the tie between the *gokenin* and the "lord of Kamakura" became less and less personal, more and more formal. The descendants of the original *gokenin* could inherit the status and obligations of their forebears, but not their emotions. They were increasingly inclined to place their own interests above those of the bakufu. The loosening of the vassal's tie with Kamakura was frequently accompanied by the loosening of ties with his kinsmen as well. It was difficult to maintain cohesion within the vassal families, particularly when their branches were separated geographically or when a branch house grew as powerful as the main family. The chain of command from the shogun to the members of the *gokenin* families, which had functioned effectively in the early days of the bakufu, had therefore weakened in its two most important links. Added to this breakdown of the authority structure was the growing impoverishment of many *gokenin* families. The burden of providing guard duty at Kamakura or Kyoto, luxurious spending habits, expansion of family size, and division of the family landholdings forced many of them into debt. The *gokenin* often mortgaged their lands to warriors who were not vassals of the bakufu or to those who were not even warriors at all. Thus many *gokenin* were unable to respond to calls for military service or financial assistance from the bakufu.

The decline of the Kamakura government accelerated after two invasion attempts by the Mongols in 1274 and 1281. The bakufu was able to muster military forces to fend off both, but its success spawned much warrior discontent, especially in the west, where bakufu control had never been complete. In meeting the Mongol threat the Kamakura government had relied on the military support not only of the *gokenin*, but of other local warriors as well. Many warriors who had used their own resources to build up and man the defenses at the main point of the Mongol attack in Kyushu demanded rewards for their efforts. Since no land or booty could be confiscated from the seaborne Mongols, the bakufu had to resort to a number of other devices to satisfy its supporters. It sometimes expropriated estate proprietorships from the court aristocracy on the pretense of defective titles, or it divided income from the office of land steward among several claimants. But even by manipulating these resources, the bakufu failed to meet all the claims, and finally in 1294 it was forced to declare that there would be no more granting of rewards for service in the campaigns of 1274 and 1281. Coupled with the waning loyalty of the *gokenin*, the resulting economic discontent among the warrior class left the bakufu highly vulnerable to internal rebellion.

The overthrow of the Kamakura government finally came in 1334. It was prompted by the anachronistic ambitions of the Emperor Go-Daigo (1288–1339), who hoped to reestablish the long-dead practice of direct imperial rule. Quixotic though Go-

Daigo's scheme may have been, many of the great warrior chieftains throughout the country, anxious to break free of bakufu control, rallied to his cause when he called for its overthrow in 1333. So weakened was Kamakura's base of support that within a few months the bakufu collapsed, and the leaders of the Hōjō family were stripped of power. The attempted restoration of the imperial government, however, proved unsuccessful. Real power lay not in the hands of Go-Daigo but with the warrior magnates who had made his revolt a success. Seizing the opportunity provided by the overthrow of the Hōjō, one of these powerful warrior leaders, Ashikaga Takauji (1305–1358), forced the emperor to abdicate in 1336 and had himself named shogun by Go-Daigo's successor.

Ashikaga Takauji was not able to impose on the warrior class the same sort of discipline that Yoritomo had. The new bakufu, established in the Muromachi section of Kyoto, never acquired a firm base of power because the collapse of Go-Daigo's restoration movement led to civil war within the country. The ostensible cause of the war was the existence of two rival imperial courts. In 1336, after being deposed by Takauji, Go-Daigo fled to the mountainous region near Yoshino (see map) and established a court there to challenge the authority of his successor at Kyoto. For the next six decades, the bakufu-supported northern court at the capital and the southern court at Yoshino, each claiming the right to the throne, waged sporadic warfare. The issue of dynastic succession was of little importance to most of the local warriors who joined the armies of the two courts; they were interested in the opportunities that civil strife provided for expanding landholdings. If one warrior leader decided to cast his lot with the northern court, it was often because his neighbor was fighting for the southern court. Similarly, if the general of an opposing force held out the promise of rewards to a warrior fighting for the opposite side, the warrior would often switch sides in the midst of a campaign. Each warrior family tried to make the best deal it could. Some families even took care that its members be on both sides, so that the family would not lose no matter what the outcome of the war. The cumulative effect of these local struggles was to hasten the drift toward political decentralization by weakening the estate system and by increasing the power of the bakufu-appointed provincial constables.

THE DECLINE OF THE ESTATE SYSTEM

The estate system had already begun to deteriorate before the collapse of the bakufu. With the posting of land stewards and provincial constables in the late twelfth century, the door was open to attacks by the local warrior class on the rights of the estate proprietors, who were vulnerable to encroachment because they were absentee landlords. The men who occupied the land, the estate managers and more particularly the land stewards, grew less and less willing to collect rents for aristocratic proprietors leading a life of idleness in the capital. Since these local men occupied the land, supervised the peasantry directly, and held the legal power to collect revenues from the estate, they had considerable leverage to appropriate land rights to themselves at the expense of the proprietors. The result was constant dispute between the local warriors and the absentee estate proprietors or protectors.

There were many means by which the local warriors made inroads on the rights of the aristocracy. Frequently the land steward would become a kind of tax farmer for the estate proprietor by contracting to pay him a fixed amount of revenue from the estate every year. This practice was very common at the beginning of the Kamakura bakufu, when the new regime wanted to provide financial reward for its vassals. But the land steward would often abuse his position by seizing direct control of the estate and refusing to send the rents to the proprietor. The courts at Kamakura were flooded with suits by dispossessed proprietors against the land stewards. Frequently the bakufu would solve these disputes by mediating agreements under which the recalcitrant land steward would pay back the rents on which he had reneged. By the thirteenth century a much more common arrangement was simply to divide the estate into two parts, giving full control over one half to the land steward, who thereby became a full proprietor himself.

With the outbreak of civil war in the fourteenth century, the estate system suffered increasing inroads. The warrior generals on both sides were under constant pressure to find means of rewarding their followers, and the estates of the absentee aristocrats were easy prizes to distribute. Both the bakufu and the Yoshino court adopted the practice of raising foraging taxes (*hanzei*) on certain estates to support the war effort. Half the rents of the estates were appropriated to the use of the local warriors, cutting into the rights and income of the proprietors. What began as a temporary expedient soon became a permanent and common practice. In 1368 the bakufu issued a law empowering the constables to collect half the income from all the estates in the country save those belonging to the imperial family, the Fujiwara regents, and certain religious institutions. Similarly, the bakufu often simply expropriated estates belonging to the aristocracy or large religious institutions and gave them as rewards to its victorious generals.

The assault of the warriors on the estate system accelerated during the late fourteenth century. The aristocracy, which had already lost its political power in the provinces, now lost its economic power as well. Descendants of once powerful and wealthy aristocratic families were reduced to relative poverty. Conversely, the decline of the estate system as a form of landholding strengthened the position of the local warrior class. With the destruction of the *shiki* of the absentee estate proprietors, the local warrior had more complete control over the land. He no longer had to share its revenues with holders higher up in the hierarchy of rights, and he could use the entire wealth of the land for his own purposes. Normally this meant equipping himself or attracting followers. Transactions in land became largely a matter of transferring land from one warrior to another with little reference to the original estate proprietors or even the bakufu. The real test of ownership was not an estate charter but the ability of the holder to protect himself against encroachment, and the best means of demonstrating this ability was armed occupancy of the land.

The willingness of the bakufu to sanction the destruction of the rights of estate proprietors had the effect of weakening the respect of the local warrior class for authority in general. Since it was so easy to trample on the rights of the aristocrats, there were few checks but that of superior military force on defiance of other kinds of central authority. As a result, the local warrior class of the fourteenth and fifteenth centuries was far less controllable and far more independent than that of earlier centuries. Fiercely attached to their land and sensitive primarily to the interests of their own locality, they were increasingly referred to as *kokujin* (local men) or *ji-samurai* (landed warriors). The local warriors of a particular region would often band together in temporary leagues to protect themselves against outside intrusion or to revolt against the bakufu's representatives. The provincial constables were hard pressed to bring them under any systematic control, and if they were able to do so at all it was because they were powerful militarily, not because they represented legally constituted authority.

THE RISE OF THE PROVINCIAL CONSTABLE

Just as the wars of the fourteenth century accelerated the destruction of the estate system, they also enhanced the power of the provincial constables. During the Kamakura period, the constables had been kept under close control by the bakufu. The general policy of the Hōjō regents had been to prevent the constable from using his office to acquire too much personal power. Whenever possible, the bakufu assigned constables to provinces where they had no ancestral roots or landholdings. Moreover, despite a tendency for the office to become hereditary, the bakufu reserved to itself the right to dismiss and reappoint constables at its own pleasure. Although not entirely successful, this policy seems to have resulted in keeping the constables in check.

The collapse of the Kamakura bakufu and the onset of civil war altered this situation considerably, for the constable became the main intermediary between the Ashikaga shoguns and the rest of the warrior class. When Ashikaga Takauji became shogun he began to appoint many of his kin, the heads of branch families or collateral houses of the Ashikaga, to the office of constable. In areas where a powerful local family already held sway, he often confirmed the local magnate's power by granting him the office. It was through the constables that the early Ashikaga shoguns attempted to wage the civil war. During the course of the war the new bakufu delegated considerable power to the provincial constable. In addition to his original duties and those he had taken over from the provincial governors, he was now given the power to raise taxes both on estate land and on what little public domain remained, to enforce the settlement of local land disputes, to receive confiscated lands, and to carry out other judicial functions. All these powers could be exercised for the sake of the bakufu, but they were equally useful to the constable for the expansion of his own landholdings and personal power. Given the lack of the strong vassalage tie that bound the original constables to Yoritomo, the fourteenth-century constable usually looked after his own interests rather than those of the shogun.

Backed by his official powers and sustained by extensive landholdings, the constable frequently attempted to convert the local warriors within his province into personal vassals. He was not always successful, since many of the warriors had gained considerable independence through local warfare and the expropriation of estates. But it was not uncommon for a constable to win over a body of followers through his power to raise an army in time of war or, more usually, through his judicial power to protect old land rights or grant new ones. Often he would redistribute the *shiki* to confiscated estates or grant the right to raise foraging taxes from local estates. Similarly, the constable would often establish members of branch families as landholders within his province or contract marriage ties with unrelated families to swell the ranks of his following.

By the end of the civil war in 1392, although some modicum of civil order was restored, Japan was a much less unified state than it had been under the Kamakura bakufu. The Ashikaga shoguns could rely neither on the services of bureaucratic officials nor on a national network of loyal vassals. Their power rested on an uneasy alliance with the constable families, who not only exercised nearly autonomous control over the provinces under their supervision, but monopolized most of the high offices in the bakufu administrative structure. The political structure of the Muromachi bakufu was much like the West Frankish kingdom that emerged after the collapse of the Carolingian empire. In theory, of course, the constables owed allegiance to the shogun who appointed them, and indeed many of them were from branch families of the Ashikaga line. But in practice it seems clear that the constables treated the shogun less as their lord than as a slightly more prestigious equal. They felt free to interfere with the succession of the shogunal line, and in 1441 one of the leading constables, nursing a personal grievance, even arranged the assassination of the incumbent shogun. However, none of the constables attempted to usurp or overthrow the power of the bakufu. Their own authority rested in large measure on the legal sanction of the shogun, and overthrowing him would threaten their own power. But, more important, there was little to be gained by deposing the head of the bakufu, for the landholdings of the constables were usually comparable to those of the shogun, if not more extensive. In any case, it is unlikely that an attempt at usurpation by one constable would have been tolerated by the others.

The balance of power between the constables, the bakufu, and the local warrior class was not a stable one, however. For one thing, the constables were not feudal lords in undisputed control of the provinces they nominally governed. They did not hold complete proprietary rights over the land in their provinces; nor did they command the allegiance of all the local warriors. Their landholdings often were scattered over several provinces. Moreover, the constables were unable to involve themselves directly in local affairs. Most of them maintained residences in the provinces as well as in Kyoto, but after the close of the civil war in 1392, they usually remained in the capital, either because they were reluctant to lose their influence there or because they were in charge of more than one province. Instead of governing directly, they relied on local deputies, sometimes selected from branch families, to see to the local administration. The relative weakness of their grip on local affairs meant that the constables constantly had to guard against rebellious local warrior families who chafed at outside interference in their affairs and who were as ready to cast off the constables' authority as they were to usurp the land rights of the absentee estate proprietors.

At the same time, there were potent tensions within the constable families themselves. By the fourteenth century the practice of equal inheritance had been abandoned in the upper reaches of warrior society. One son was chosen as heir of both the family headship and all the family holdings. The advantages of this practice were obvious, since it meant the wealth and power of the family could be transmitted over several generations without diminution. But the principle for deciding who would be the heir was by no means fixed. The result was the outbreak of frequent disputes within families. Brother turned against brother, uncle against nephew, and even father against son in armed struggles over the family headship. In provinces under the control of a constable family, these succession disputes often had reverberations: local warriors would throw their support behind one or the other of the disputants, and constables in neighboring provinces would often interfere as well.

By the mid-fifteenth century, these political and

social instabilities had paved the way for a new outbreak of civil disorder, the Ōnin War of 1467–1477.
Like the struggle between the northern and the southern courts, the overt cause of the war was a succession dispute. The shogun, Ashikaga Yoshimasa (1435–
1490), found himself in the difficult position of
having two heirs. Initially childless, he formally announced in 1464 that the succession would pass to his
brother, a Buddhist monk, who renounced his vows
to prepare for this future responsibility. A year later
Yoshimasa's wife bore him a son and quite naturally
insisted that he be made heir. Caught between these
two pressures, Yoshimasa remained immobile. His
ambitious wife then called on the leader of the Yamana, a powerful constable family, to support the
candidacy of her son. This prompted the Hosokawa,
another constable family long jealous of the Yamana's
power, to support the rival candidate. During the
mid-1460s both the Yamana and the Hosokawa began
to gather allies among other constable families and
the local warrior class, who seized on the dispute at
the capital as an opportunity to settle local disputes
of their own. In 1467 open warfare broke out in
Kyoto between the two opposing forces, and for
nearly a decade the region around the capital was
rent by fighting.

The Ōnin War was as important a turning point
in Japanese history as the Gempei War or the struggle
between the northern and southern courts. It destroyed the last traces of effective central power in
Japan. The capital at Kyoto, fought over, looted, and
burned time after time, was left in ruins. The estates
of the imperial family were seized by local warriors or
their chieftains, and the private exchequer of the
throne became impoverished. The aristocracy, who
had already seen their landholdings diminished by the
encroachments of the warriors, now found their very
lives endangered. Many fled to the provinces to live
on what lands they might have left. The vestigial
authority of the Ashikaga shoguns was destroyed.
Yoshimasa, a broken man, retreated from politics, and
his successors were as weak and ineffectual as the

aristocracy whose ways they aped. But most important, the war exhausted the energy and resources of the provincial constable families. Although many of them were able to preserve their landholdings, the local warrior class took the occasion of the war and its chaotic aftermath to rebel against their authority. Within the course of a generation most of the constable families had sunk into relative obscurity, and the powers they once exercised as deputies of the shogun were increasingly absorbed by a new breed of feudal magnates who sprang from the ranks of the local warrior class. The struggle among these magnates was to dominate the century following the Ōnin War, a period usually known as the "era of the warring states."

THE DAIMYO AT WAR   The novelty of the "warring states" period was not so much the prevalence of provincial warfare, which had been endemic since the fall of the Kamakura bakufu, but the emergence of consolidated territorial domains under the control of local feudal lords or barons called *daimyō*.* Unlike the chieftains of the pre-Kamakura warrior alliances or the provincial constables, the daimyo owed his position not to the legal sanction of the imperial government or the bakufu, but to the force of arms. He was a power unto himself. The emperor and the shogun continued to survive at Kyoto, but the daimyo had little respect for any power but that won on the battlefield. His domain was pieced together through warfare against his neighbors and was protected against their encroachments by his army of vassals. In effect, it was a tiny garrison state.

By 1500 the country was divided under the control of two or three hundred daimyo, the most powerful holding sway over areas as large as one of the old im-

---

* The term *daimyō*, literally "great name," was originally used to refer to holders of many rice fields (*myō*), in contrast to holders of few (*shōmyō* or "small names"). During the sixteenth century, it was one of many terms applied to the larger feudal lords, but modern historians have found it convenient to refer to them only by this term.

perial provinces. The weaker, hardly more powerful than the castellans of feudal Europe, controlled only small and easily defended river valleys or basins. Although a few daimyo were descended from the old provincial constable families, the majority of them sprang from relatively humble origins. Some belonged to families that had served as local deputies for the constables, and others belonged to the ordinary local warrior class. The number of daimyo was by no means fixed, nor was the size of their domains. Domain boundaries shifted with the fortunes of war, and daimyo rose and fell with sudden swiftness. Mobility among the warrior class was enormous. Since this mobility often depended on the betrayal of one's nominal lord or master, some later Japanese historians characterized the period as an era of "insubordination" (*gekokujo,* literally "the overthrow of those above by those below"). One Western historian, reflecting this view, has called the ascendancy of the daimyo "the golden age of turncoats and mediocrities."

Despite the constant rise and fall of the daimyo and the fluctuations in their power, the methods by which they governed were relatively constant. Every daimyo had to rule with and through his vassals. It was they who fought beside him to protect or expand his domain, and it was to them that he looked for aid in maintaining order. The nucleus of the daimyo's power, and the base on which the stability of the domain rested, was therefore his vassal band.

In contrast to the warrior bands of earlier times, the vassal band of the daimyo generally was not recruited from among kinsmen. To be sure, the daimyo looked to his kinsmen for help, but with the spreading practice of indivisible inheritance, the heir to the family headship and land was far more powerful economically and politically than the kinsmen belonging to his generation. Those who did not inherit the family lands could no longer count themselves the peers of the family head. They were merely the highest ranking (but by no means the most dependable) of his followers. The daimyo was therefore far more a feudal lord and far less a family patriarch than the great warrior chieftains of the eleventh and twelfth centuries. Although the term "housemen" (*kenin*) was still applied to the daimyo's followers, it was far more common to refer to them as "house vassals" (*kashin*), "hereditary retainers" (*fudai*), or "direct vassals" (*jikishin*). The term "ally" (*tozama*) was also used to denote those of the daimyo's followers who were subdued by him in battle, but who were not so closely tied to him as the rest of the vassal band. The use of these terms reflected a greater emphasis on personal service than on family ties.

Unlike the members of early warrior bands, the vassals of the daimyo, whether traditionally retainers of his family or brought under his sway by conquest, normally made a formal pledge of allegiance to him. Usually they would sign or affix their personal seals to written oaths of loyalty. This practice had precedents even in Kamakura times, but it had become more uniform and widespread by the fifteenth century. The use of loyalty oaths reflected the fact that vassalage had become more formal than the loyalty ties of earlier centuries. What the eleventh- and twelfth-century warriors had been content to let rest on mutual confidence and personal emotion now was clothed in the legal trappings of a formal document sworn before a host of deities. The oath of allegiance became primarily a means of identifying vassals, not a guarantee of their service.

The vassalage tie was usually cemented by the granting of a fief or stipend from the daimyo. Since the estate system had collapsed as a system of landholding, grants were made not of land rights (*shiki*), but of the land itself. The concept of *chigyō*, or physical occupancy of the land, replaced the concept of *shiki*, or rights to income from the land, as the primary concept of landholding. In many ways, this innovation resembled the *seisin* concept in European feudal land law. Although not the same as absolute ownership, the *chigyō* form of possession was much more complete than the holding of a *shiki*. The grant or confirmation of a fief was made for a specified area measured in standard units and assessed at a specific value either in rice or in money. The vassal who received land had no obligation to forward part of the harvest to his lord, and he could divide it up among his own retainers. Whenever possible, the daimyo tried to keep the fief under the direct control of the vassal. The vassal was not free to sell his fief, since this would weaken his ability to fight for the daimyo. At the same time, vassals were usually encouraged to abandon the practice of equal inheritance if they had not already done so, and women, who could not fight, were forbidden to inherit land. All these practices, of course, were similar to those that arose at the height of feudal society in Europe.

In return for the grant of a fief, the vassal had the obligation of rendering military service to the daimyo. In contrast to Kamakura times, when no limits had been placed on the amount of service the *gokenin* owed to the bakufu, a vassal of the daimyo usually owed military service in proportion to the size of his fief. Although there was no uniform rate throughout the country, the larger daimyo usually kept records showing that a vassal holding a piece of land worth so many pieces of gold or silver was required in time of war to provide so many horsemen, so many spears, so many standard bearers, so many baggage carriers, and so forth. The vassals were also expected to be in a state of constant readiness. Some daimyo held regular inspections of their vassals' equipment once or twice a year.

Since the fief was held on the condition of military service, the vassalage tie was more contractual than it had been in earlier times. It was also much less one-sided. Vassals who refused to provide military service to the daimyo, who were tardy in doing so, or who showed the slightest sign of disloyalty met with punishment. But by the same token a daimyo who failed to protect his vassals, either because he was unwilling or unable to do so, risked betrayal. The mutuality of the lord-vassal tie made the relationship far less stable than the more primitive bonds that held together the early warrior bands. Treachery was common and often profitable to vassals promised larger fiefs or stipends by the rivals of their lord. Despite the constant protestation that loyalty was the highest virtue, the vassalage tie was tinged with suspicion and uneasiness. A Jesuit missionary who visited Japan in the sixteenth century commented that one of the great shortcomings of the Japanese was the lack of loyalty by vassals to their lords:

They rebel against them whenever they have a chance, either usurping them or joining with their enemies. Then they about-turn and declare themselves friends again, only to rebel once more when the opportunity presents itself; yet this sort of conduct does not discredit them at all. As a result, none of the lords (or very few of them) are secure in their domains and, as we can see, there are many upheavals and wars.*

The reason for this state of affairs was that loyalty had become a matter of self-interest rather than an ethical imperative.

At the same time, however, there never developed in Japan the practice of multiple homages that figured so prominently in European feudalism. In Europe an ambitious knight would often make himself the vassal of several lords in order to acquire new fiefs. He was then, of course, legally obligated to render military service to several lords at once. To avoid confusion, his primary duty was held to be toward his original lord, who was designated as his liege lord. But he often established liege homages with his other lords as well. Although a Japanese vassal might betray his lord, he did not serve two lords at once, and no legal forms developed to accommodate him if he wanted to. Given the instability of the vassalage bond and the prevalence of betrayal in fifteenth- and sixteenth-century Japan, it is difficult to explain this difference from the European case, as many historians have done, by attributing a greater degree of moral force to the tie of vassalage in Japan. A far

---

* Michael Cooper (ed.), *They Came to Japan* (Berkeley, Calif.: University of California Press, 1965), p. 46.

simpler and more convincing explanation is that the Japanese vassal never regarded the feudal bond as a source of income but as primarily a guarantee of his security. When his lord failed to provide him protection, he simply looked for a new one.

The daimyo and his vassals engaged in a style of warfare much different from that of earlier times. Success in battle came to depend less on individual prowess and skill than on the ability to organize large masses of fighting men. Armies were more strictly organized than those of earlier centuries. In time of war, the daimyo usually divided his vassal band into distinct military commands much like those of a modern army with its hierarchy of divisions, regiments, battalions, and companies. The larger or more trustworthy vassals, often designated as generals (*taishō*) or captains (*shō*), were made commanders of these fighting units. They issued or transmitted orders to the rest of the vassals (*ki,* or knights) and their subvassals (*yoriki,* or knight's retainers). Equally significant, the armies of the daimyo relied on foot soldiers (*ashigaru*) as much as on mounted warriors. Foot troops wore light armor and were armed with spears and similar implements rather than the nobler sword or bow. Recruited from the peasantry, they often made up the bulk of the army. According to surviving records of one powerful daimyo who mobilized about 5,500 men on his domain, 3,600 of his forces were spearmen and only 556 were horsemen. The reason for this change in the technology of war is obvious. As the injunctions of one daimyo of the late fourteenth century put it, "A sword worth ten thousand pieces can be overcome by one hundred spears worth only one hundred pieces." The foot soldier was not only less expensive to maintain, but in massed formations he could vanquish the proud horsemen who had so long dominated Japanese history. Even more ominous for the traditional style of fighting was the introduction of the musket by the Portuguese in the 1540s. The new weapon was seized upon with great alacrity by the contending daimyo, and by the last quarter of the century the more powerful of them, significantly the most successful, were beginning to organize units of musketeers conscripted from the peasantry.

The development of new offensive tactics was paralleled by the growth of new defensive measures. The age of the daimyo was also an age of castle building. Although the idea of a fortified stronghold was not new to the warrior class, the chronic character of warfare, the use of foot soldiers, and the attendant insecurity of life accelerated the development of military architecture. "The landed families of each village and district now build fortifications and erect castles," recorded the chronicler of one daimyo family. "Day and night they must exert constant vigilance." Early castles were usually rude hilltop retreats surrounded by simple palisades or ramparts. Gradually there developed a style of castle building which, admitting differing traditions of architectural style, was remarkably similar to that of late feudal Europe. At the center of the castle was a tower, much like the European *donjon,* which commanded a view of the surrounding countryside and served as the ultimate retreat in case, of attack. Surrounding the castle were a series of outerworks or walls designed to provide strategic positions to fend off an attacking force. Frequently, if the castle was not on a hilltop, it was located by a lake, a pond, or a stream or river whose waters could be diverted into a moat too wide and deep to be waded across.

Often there would be branch castles and fortifications on the boundaries of the domain as well to provide protection for those vassals living too far from the main castle and to form a first line of defense for the domain. The vassals of the daimyo were usually assigned to garrison or defend the castle closest to their own fiefs, but by the late sixteenth century some daimyo required their vassals to live close by the castle rather than on their own land.

THE DAIMYO   The daimyo domain began primarily as a local defen-
AT PEACE   sive unit that grew out of the original vassal band, but increasingly it became an administrative unit as well.

Even in an age dominated by warfare and violence, political power could not be stabilized solely by success on the battlefield. In his struggles to maintain and expand his domain, the daimyo had to act not merely as feudal lord, but also as territorial ruler. By the early sixteenth century, many of the daimyo began to develop administrative regimes to consolidate their control over the people and to make the exploitation of their wealth more efficient. The administrative consolidation of the domains was sometimes aided by the fact that the daimyo inherited by default the legal powers of the constable, but more usually it grew out of his own pragmatic experience.

It was symptomatic of the growing political character of the daimyo domain that, by the late fifteenth century, there began to emerge a body of private domainal law. Many daimyo families developed "house codes" over the course of a generation or two. The earliest example of these were the "wall writings" of the Ōuchi family, a document of fifty articles pieced together between 1439 and 1495. By the sixteenth century most other daimyo families had them as well. The house codes were often modeled on the provisions of the Jōei Formulary of 1232 or other long-standing pieces of bakufu legislation, but usually they were highly local in character. Their provisions included not only scraps of bakufu law, but ancestral family injunctions, local legal practices, and administrative rules required by the peculiarities of the region. The provisions of the house codes applied only to the warriors and peasants of the daimyo's own domain; they did not apply to the population of his neighbor. Moreover, beyond the daimyo there was no higher court of appeal. The only alternatives to submitting to his decisions were to betray him if one were a warrior or to escape to a neighboring domain if one were a peasant. The daimyo domain became a unitary legal jurisdiction, and the daimyo its chief judge and legislator.

The daimyo domain became a strong economic unit as well. Faced with the burden of constant military preparedness, most daimyo were anxious to control and exploit the landed wealth of their domains as best they could. Failure to do this, of course, had been one of the reasons for the downfall of the constable families, who were cut off from direct control of the land. For a daimyo who had established the boundaries of his domain on the battlefield, the collection of revenue from its land became one of his primary goals.

Initially, of course, most daimyo had subsisted on their own landholdings. During the late fifteenth and early sixteenth centuries, the domain of the daimyo was usually divided between his own demesne, the fiefs of his vassals, and the subfiefs of their retainers. Each collected rents from the peasantry, sometimes in rice and sometimes in cash. But by the second quarter of the sixteenth century, many daimyo who were anxious to enlarge their wealth began to levy taxes on all the land within their domains. To accomplish this, they carried out land surveys and kept registers showing the size, location, and condition of land within the area under their control. This enabled the daimyo to determine who was responsible for military service and who was responsible for paying land taxes. By the latter part of the century, the registers were also put to other uses, such as determining the obligation of peasants to perform labor or military service. The revival of land surveys and regular tax collection made land tenure more secure for the peasantry, but, more important, it marked the reestablishment of administrative stability at the local level.

The collection of regular land taxes brought the peasantry far more closely under the control of the daimyo than they had been under either the old estate proprietors or the provincial constables. The peasant village, rather than the estate, became the basic unit of administration within the domain. The village was placed under the control of a village headman, usually one of the more well-to-do peasants, who often received tax exemption or a small stipend for his services. A vassal of the daimyo was often appointed as a deputy over a group of villages, and it was through him that orders were transmitted to the village heads. The village head, although obliged to transmit these orders to the villagers, was given the freedom to carry them out in whatever way he saw fit. Although this system gave local administration a certain amount of flexibility, the village headmen could not stray too far from the daimyo's orders, since most daimyo held the villagers collectively responsible not only for criminal and other offenses, but also for payment of taxes. If the peasants tried to flee from the village, refused to pay taxes, or evaded other obligations the daimyo exacted from them, the whole village was threatened with punishment. However offensive this might seem to our notions of individual responsibility and guilt, it was an effective means of mobilizing community pressure behind the maintenance of local order. The result of all these measures was a countryside that was more tightly controlled than in previous centuries, yet one that was administered by a relatively small administrative staff.

The daimyo also realized that increasing the wealth of their domains was as important as controlling it. As warfare became larger in scale, the daimyo needed the wherewithal to supply his men with food, weapons, and other supplies, as well as a disciplined chain of command and a gift for strategy. Many of them began to increase their economic strength by bringing new land into cultivation and amassing bullion. They reclaimed marginal land, built complex irrigation works, and constructed embankments to prevent flood disasters. The work of these projects was provided by labor corvées levied on the peasantry, and many of the reclaimed fields and the canals and dikes built by the daimyo are in use today. Similarly, those daimyo fortunate enough to find deposits of metal ore on their domains, particularly iron, gold, and silver, promoted the development of mining. Not coincidentally, the fifteenth and sixteenth centuries saw the development of new techniques for refining precious metals and ore which made possible a more efficient use of these mineral resources. The necessity of fueling the engine of war brought a burst of economic development in the daimyo regimes.

But no matter how astute the daimyo were in exploiting the natural resources of their domains, none could be completely self-sufficient. Consequently, many daimyo began to adopt a policy of free trade within their domains to attract merchants. In earlier centuries the production and sale of most manufactured goods, and of many scarce goods, had been under the control of local monopoly associations (*za*) operating under charters bought from estate proprietors. The daimyo abolished these old monopoly privileges and established open markets in their domains. All merchants were allowed to trade, and no taxes were collected on the trade. Often the daimyo would encourage the merchants to settle permanently in their castle towns in hopes that they could provide the scarce necessities the daimyo needed. By the sixteenth century, some were designated "official purveyors" (*goyōshōnin*); they served as quartermasters for the daimyo's army, carried local produce to large market towns outside the domain to be traded for other goods, and supervised the financial affairs of the domain. Since the role of these men was often more political than economic, they were frequently recruited from the warrior class or the more well-to-do peasantry, as well as from the merchant class.

The ability of the daimyo to raise revenue from nonfeudal sources meant that he did not have to resort to raising money from his vassals. In Europe, local lords pursued the practice of collecting various kinds of feudal levies. When a feudal lord was faced with unusual expenses such as the payment of ransom, the knighting of his eldest son, or the marriage of his daughter, he would often levy payment of feudal aids (occasional levies of money) from his vassals. Similarly, he often required the heir of a vassal to pay a fee when he inherited the fief held by his father. And, as mercenary armies became common, he often allowed his vassals to buy their way out of military service by a payment known as scutage, or army aid. In Japan, by contrast, if the daimyo needed more income, he found it easier to raise it by some means other than squeezing his vassals. The feudal bond remained for him, as for his vassals, primarily military and political in character. It was a means of raising an army and protecting his domain, not a means of raising revenue. The granting of fiefs or stipends to vassals therefore never eroded the vassalage tie as it often did in late feudal Europe. It was only with the advent of peace in the seventeenth century, when the vassal's services as a fighting man were no longer needed by the daimyo, that the income provided by a fief or stipend became more important than the physical security it provided.

*   *   *

The political map of Japan during the "warring states" period was no less fragmented than that of Europe during "high" feudalism, but in many ways it was less complex. Since the warrior served only one lord at a time and since the vassalage bond was never diluted by the financial needs of the lord, there did not evolve the intricate webs of vassal ties that characterized many parts of Europe. The bounds of political jurisdiction were also much clearer. There were fewer ambiguities as to who controlled a given piece of territory or who was to receive taxes from the peasants of a particular village. On the whole, feudal government in Japan was much neater than in the European case. Perhaps as a result, it was easier to unify Japan than it was to create the modern nations of Western Europe.

Chapter 5

From
Feudal Anarchy to
National
Unity

In Europe, national histories developed in two main directions at the close of the feudal era. In England and France there emerged unified monarchical states in which the king asserted his powers as supreme feudal overlord to curb his warring vassals and arbitrate disputes between them to the advantage of the crown. In Germany, where the emperor attempted to convert the feudal hierarchy into a political chain of command, feudal anarchy was followed by the formation of numerous small states more or less independent of the central authority. In both cases feudal practices were used to reconstitute centralized political authority, and feudal suzerainty was converted into territorial sovereignty.

In Japan, a balance was achieved between these two tendencies. The new political order that emerged in the seventeenth century placed a supreme feudal monarch, the shogun, over a large number of small semiautonomous territorial states headed by daimyo. For historians accustomed to the European feudal experience, particularly that of England and France, this is a confusing situation. It has led many of them to describe the new political order in Japan as "centralized feudalism." But since the absence of effective central authority is one of the key aspects of a feudal political system, "centralized feudalism" is a contradiction in terms. It would be far simpler, and far more accurate, to think of the new political system as a hybrid state held together by feudal bonds at the top and by bureaucratic means at the bottom.

REUNIFICATION For all the divisiveness of the country under the daimyo, it was they who laid the foundations for the reunification of the country. They had created efficient local regimes and kept the countryside under far better control than either the imperial government or the bakufu had ever been able to do. It took no great leap of imagination for an individual daimyo to conceive of uniting the country into a single domain using the same methods by which he had built up his own domain. By the 1560s, many daimyo harbored ambitions of conquest beyond the shifting boundaries of their domains. The consolidating and expanding of local domains soon turned into a process of national military unification, and within the space of a generation or so the country was once again brought under central control.

The relative speed with which unification was accomplished is not easy to account for. Perhaps part of the answer lies in the continuing strength of a tradition of national unity even during the period of feudal anarchy. Despite their poverty and military weakness, both the emperor and the shogun survived in Kyoto as potent reminders that in former times the country had been under central rule, and in some cases the daimyo had sought the honors and offices that they could still bestow. Part of the answer might also be that the Japanese continued to have before them the example of a unified central state in China. Many of the sixteenth-century daimyo, if not learned men or even literate, were familiar with early Chinese political thought, which revolved mainly on the problem of how to create political unity and social peace. But doubtless the key factor was Japan's geography. Unlike the embryonic monarchies of late feudal Europe, her boundaries were clearly defined by the seas that surrounded her, and her isolation kept her free from the foreign interference or invasion that might have impeded her reunification. The islands formed a natural geopolitical unit, and their conquest from within was a manageable goal.

The task of unification was not accomplished by one of the great daimyo houses that had emerged by the mid-sixteenth century, but was the work of three relatively obscure men—Nobunaga, Hideyoshi, and Ieyasu—none of whom was a major figure on the national scene in 1560. Their obscurity may have helped them succeed where the great daimyo failed. For one thing, it meant that they began their careers with few powerful enemies. For another, it gave them the advantage of surprise. In any case, it is clear that they took advantage of the struggles among the large daimyo to build their own power, and eventually were able to bring these daimyo under their sway.

The first of the three great unifiers of the late sixteenth century was Oda Nobunaga (1534–1582), the son of a minor daimyo whose domains were located in central Japan. A rough and ruthless man, Nobunaga began his rise in 1560 when, at the head of a small band of vassals, he successfully ambushed and routed an expedition against Kyoto by his powerful and ambitious neighbor Imagawa Yoshitomo (1519–1560). Allying with the enemies of Imagawa and certain daimyo on his own flanks, he began to build a strong consolidated domain athwart the main route through central Honshu between Kyoto in the west and the Kantō plain in the east. That he had larger ambitions is clear. In 1567 he built a strong fortified headquarters at Gifu, named in memory of the place from which one of the legendary rulers of China had begun his conquest of the country, and for his personal seal he chose the motto "The whole country under one military power." By 1568 he had managed to secure military control of the ancient capital at Kyoto, and five years later he felt confident enough to depose the incumbent shogun, Ashikaga Yoshiaki (1537–1597), bringing a formal end to the Muromachi bakufu. During the 1570s he campaigned ceaselessly in central Japan, turning his armies against both the daimyo of the region and certain powerful Buddhist religious communities near the capital.

Nobunaga's military successes rested on several factors. First of all, his location in the central part of Honshu prevented the powerful daimyo families in the west from allying with those of the east. Second, he was one of the first military leaders in Japan to make effective use of firearms, and on one occasion at least the superiority of his firepower carried the day in battle. Third, he was an astute strategist and tactician. He was careful in choosing his enemies, and avoided taking on more than one main rival at a time. Perhaps most important of all, he was careful to consolidate his military victories by winning the support of the vassals or enemies of his rivals through the grant or confirmation of their fiefs. The stamp of Nobunaga's vermilion seal on land grants was a guarantee that he would protect the holder against rival claimants. After the death of the last shogun, Nobunaga's seal was perhaps the most potent sanction of land rights in the country. The first steps toward military unification were thus an extension of the feudal politics by which the local daimyo had extended their domains.

Nobunaga met a premature and untimely end by the hand of one of his vassals, but the momentum of unification continued under his able lieutenant, Hideyoshi (1536–1598). A man so humble in origin that he was born without a surname, Hideyoshi had won a reputation as one of Nobunaga's ablest generals. As Nobunaga's successor, he won the loyal support of many of his chief's other followers and inherited much of his chief's domain. During the late 1580s, he built on this territorial core by issuing land grants to daimyo who swore allegiance to him and by conquering those who did not, such as the Mōri and the Shimazu in the west. By 1590, with the defeat of the Hōjō family, who controlled much of the Kantō region, the military unification of the country was complete. Hideyoshi received pledges of submission from all the powerful daimyo of the country, making him a military overlord of unrivaled power. All the land in the country was either part of his direct domain or granted under his seal to other daimyo. In practical terms this gave him greater political authority than any single man had been able to attain for centuries. Even Yoritomo at the height of his strength had not exercised so much power.

The hegemony of Hideyoshi, as well as the force of his land grants, derived from his demonstrated military success, but political leniency was also a key to his achievement. Like Nobunaga before him, Hideyoshi had not sought to destroy his rival daimyo: it was far simpler to convert a defeated enemy into an ally or a vassal. Moreover, an enemy who became a follower could be used to fight against new adversaries, and the lure of rewards from confiscated lands that followed a successful campaign served to bind him closer. As a practical matter, the military strength of the daimyo in the 1580s was so evenly balanced that the complete destruction of a rival was beyond the resources of even Hideyoshi himself. Only in his final campaign against the Hōjō family, when he held sway over most of central and western Japan, did he wipe out his opponent. He was able to do so then only because he could draw on the manpower provided by his many vassal daimyo. By dealing gently with former foes, Hideyoshi, like most of the successful daimyo houses, was able to consolidate the gains won on the battlefield.

Military unification, however, did not result in the immediate establishment of a stable political regime. Both Nobunaga and Hideyoshi had begun administrative and political consolidation of the territory they had conquered, but neither was able to establish a new dynasty of rulers or even a durable set of political institutions. Since Nobunaga was killed midway in his career, it is difficult to assess his policy. But there is no question that in his old age Hideyoshi dissipated the military gains he had made. While still engaged in his unification campaigns, he had shown many promising signs that he would undertake administrative innovations. He carried out extensive land surveys to bring some order to the chaotic state of landholdings in the country; issued decrees designed to separate the mass of the peasantry from the warrior class and so reduce the social mobility that caused much local disorder; and for the first time in centuries, began minting a nationwide coinage. He even sought the office of shogun from the emperor to legitimize his power. But since this office traditionally could be held only by descendants of the Minamoto, he was denied the post and had to settle for the court post of regent.

Once Hideyoshi had finished his conquest of the country, however, he undertook a series of ambitious but unsuccessful military campaigns in Korea in 1592, and again in 1597. Although his motives are obscure, there is little question that these efforts diverted him from the more important task of organizing the realm politically. Shortly before his death he sought to ensure the future of his infant heir Hideyori (1593–1615) by extracting oaths of allegiance from his principal vassals and organizing a council of five of the most powerful daimyo to act as caretakers of the country until his son came of age. But once he was gone, the careful structure of alliances on which his power rested dissolved as new struggles arose among his major vassals.

The final task of political unification was left to Tokugawa Ieyasu (1542–1616), the last of the three great unifiers of Japan. Like Nobunaga, Ieyasu sprang from a relatively minor daimyo family in central Japan, and he had been an ally and vassal of both Nobunaga and Hideyoshi. After Hideyoshi defeated the Hōjō family in 1590, he had assigned Ieyasu command of the prosperous and strategic Kantō plain, traditionally the cradle of conquest in feudal Japan. This made Ieyasu the strongest daimyo in the country next to Hideyoshi, and after Hideyoshi's death it was to him that most of Hideyoshi's former vassals rallied for leadership. With this backing, Ieyasu began to move against the powerful daimyo who had been appointed to protect the interests of Hideyoshi's heir and who were likewise ambitious to assume Hideyoshi's mantle. In 1600, at the decisive battle of

Sekigahara in the mountainous region of central Honshu, Ieyasu and his allies defeated these rivals, and the road lay clear for political unification of the country. In material terms Ieyasu was unchallenged. In addition to his own considerable direct domain, he had at his disposal the domains confiscated from his defeated enemies. Perhaps a third of all the productive land in the country was under his personal control or in the hands of his kinsmen and retainers. There was no one left who could challenge the formidable army he could raise from this land.

Endowed with a shrewd political sense, Ieyasu took a businesslike view of his military power. Rather than embark on capricious overseas ventures as Hideyoshi had, he regarded military unification as a step toward political unification. He had not forgotten what had happened to the heirs of Nobunaga and Hideyoshi, nor even those of Yoritomo, and he was determined to establish a dynasty. In 1603 he secured from the emperor the title of shogun, which gave him legal authority over the warrior class and provided formal recognition of his military ascendancy. After holding the title for two years, he abdicated in favor of his son, Hidetada (1579–1632), and spent the rest of his life constructing a political framework to perpetuate the rule of his family. Said to believe in the maxim that "every government must work by rules just as a carpenter does," Ieyasu showed an eye for sound construction. The new bakufu, which was later refined and perfected by Hidetada and his son, Iemitsu (1604–1651), was to endure for two and a half centuries.

THE EDO
BAKUFU

The new political order that emerged in the years following Sekigahara was constructed out of feudal material and mortared with feudal cement. In building the new bakufu, Ieyasu and his heirs had to contend with the fact that the military unification of the country had left most of the domains intact. Although individually the daimyo were considerably weaker than Ieyasu's formidable military machine, collectively they outnumbered the Tokugawa. Their numerical advantage made Ieyasu loath to move against them militarily. Instead, he chose to make the daimyo domains the basic building blocks of the new national regime. In bringing the daimyo under control, Ieyasu relied primarily on his own experience as a local daimyo. Indeed, the way in which he had governed his own domain became the basic blueprint for the new regime. Just as his old castle town, Edo (see map), became the new capital of the country, so did the principles by which he had controlled his retainers become the basis for his control over the subdued daimyo. The regime he created was not a unified nation-state, but a confederation of daimyo under the hegemony of the Tokugawa family held together much as Ieyasu's own vassal band had been.

After 1600 the status of daimyo was more precisely defined than it had been before: the daimyo were those followers of the Tokugawa house whose landholdings yielded over 10,000 koku of rice. The daimyo were varied in origin. Some, like the Shimazu in southern Kyushu, had been independent regional overlords for centuries. Most sprang from families that had not figured prominently on the national scene before the Ōnin War, and many were upstarts created as daimyo by Nobunaga, Hideyoshi, and Ieyasu himself. The size of their domains was also varied, ranging from those of the great lords such as the Maeda, with over one million koku in rice land, to petty daimyo who did not even have the wherewithal to support a castle. The typical daimyo, however, was one who had achieved his position by prowess on the battlefield and whose holding was a medium-size domain yielding 50,000 to 200,000 koku of rice.

As was common practice in the sixteenth century, the daimyo were divided into two main groups, *fudai* or vassal daimyo, and *tozama* or allied daimyo. This distinction, which was more the creation of custom than of law, was based principally on the criterion of political reliability. The *fudai* daimyo were considered to be the more trustworthy. Many were descended from the original vassal band of the Tokugawa family, and many had been elevated to daimyo status as a reward for their service to Ieyasu during and after the battle of Sekigahara. The *tozama* daimyo were those who had been too powerful in their own right to be considered subordinates of Ieyasu, and hence had to be regarded as allies of the Tokugawa. Many had been vassals of Hideyoshi as Ieyasu himself had been. Some of them had been Ieyasu's supporters in the battle of Sekigahara, but others had submitted to him only after defeat. In addition to these two groups, Ieyasu and his successors after 1600 created a third group, the *shimpan* or related daimyo. These daimyo were really heads of Tokugawa branch families, the first of them being Ieyasu's own sons, and were appointed to provide heirs to the office of shogun in the event that the main Tokugawa line died out.

All the daimyo, whatever their size or origin, were treated as direct vassals of the shogun. Like the retainers of a sixteenth-century feudal lord, they were bound to the shogun by pledges of personal allegiance. The daimyo as a group swore their loyalty to each shogun when he was installed in office, and when an heir succeeded to the position of daimyo, he swore an oath to the shogun and signed it in blood. In return for his loyalty pledge, the daimyo held his domain as a fief from the shogun. Even if his ancestors had won the domain on the field of battle, it still had to be confirmed by a grant from the shogun. Some historians have regarded this tie between the shogun and the daimyo as a purely legal formality, very different from the personal tie that linked the daimyo and his retainers. True though this may have been later on, the feudal character of the tie was still very strong during the early seventeenth century. Tenure of a domain was indeed precarious, dependent on the will of the shogun.

In practice as well as in theory, the shogun retained the right to transfer a daimyo from one domain to another, to reduce his domain, or to confiscate it completely. Ieyasu and his first two successors used these powers rather freely to reduce the power of the daimyo. There were several grounds on which confiscatory powers could be exercised. First of all, lands could be seized from those defeated in battle. As we have seen, Ieyasu used confiscation to humble his opponents after the battle of Sekigahara, and the same practice was followed after the defeat of Hideyoshi's son, Hideyori, who staged a revolt against the bakufu in 1615. Second, lands could be confiscated if a daimyo left no heir. It was particularly important to the shogun that a daimyo's heir be as loyal and ready to perform military service as his father, and the bakufu was extremely strict even toward the customary practice of adopting heirs in the absence of a natural one. During the reign of the first three shoguns, fifty-seven daimyo houses were extinguished for failure of heirs; many of them were *fudai* and *shimpan* daimyo as well as *tozama*. Finally, lands could be reduced or confiscated in order to censure daimyo for infractions of the bakufu's laws or for other untoward behavior. Such punitive confiscations or reductions in domain ensued for a multitude of reasons, from disorderly conduct to the insanity of the daimyo. But a common cause seems to have been family disputes over succession, and in these cases the motive behind the confiscations was less a desire to uphold the bakufu's regulations or standards of morality than to render potential enemies powerless. Rather significantly, the majority of those who suffered punitive confiscations were *tozama* daimyo.

This ruthless policy of reducing daimyo domains, which has been called by some historians "the squashing of the daimyo," had important side effects. It served to increase the landed strength of the Tokugawa family and its close allies. As a matter of policy, Ieyasu and his heirs tried to enlarge the holdings of the *fudai* daimyo, the *shimpan* daimyo, and their own domain at the expense of the *tozama* daimyo. By the middle of the seventeenth century, perhaps two-fifths of the productive land of the country had changed hands from one daimyo to another, and about one-third of the original *tozama* daimyo were completely dispossessed of their land.

The bakufu's policy of confiscation also resulted

in a drastic rearrangement of the political landscape. Following a policy Ieyasu had pursued toward his own vassals before 1600, the bakufu used its power to transfer daimyo from one domain to another. Whenever possible it tried to keep the more reliable daimyo closer to the bakufu headquarters at Edo and the less reliable separate from one another in the less accessible parts of the country. The bakufu's direct domains were consolidated in the Kantō area near Edo, and all the principal cities of the country, including both the ancient capital of Kyoto and large trading cities and ports, such as Osaka and Nagasaki, were placed under the direct control of the bakufu. The domains of the *fudai* daimyo were in the central part of the country, where they controlled key land routes or strategic mountain passes. By contrast, the *tozama* were kept in the extremities of the archipelago, in Kyushu or in the southwest and northeast regions of Honshu. By 1650 few daimyo families occupied the same lands they had held at the beginning of the century; most had been shifted at least once to new locales in order to establish a geographical balance of power within the country.

As vassals of the shogun, the daimyo had much the same obligations toward him as the sixteenth-century daimyo had required of their followers. The foremost of these was military service, including the obligation to furnish men and weapons in time of war and to help subdue rebellions. It was through the use of such feudal levies that the bakufu crushed Hideyori in 1615 and put down the Shimabara revolt in 1637–1638. The regulations of the bakufu required that the daimyo keep standing forces in readiness in proportion to the size of their domain. But military service also included the obligation to assist the bakufu in the construction of defensive fortifications. With the aid of materials and manpower supplied by the daimyo, the bakufu built the great castle at Edo, which served as its headquarters, as well as similar fortifications at Nagoya and other key areas. Many historians have suggested that this policy was designed to weaken the daimyo economically, and it did indeed have this effect, but this was not necessarily the intention of this policy. Rather, this policy was the work of those men who felt that the daimyo owed their feudal overlord material assistance as a matter of course.

The other major obligation of the daimyo was personal attendance at the shogunal court in Edo (the present city of Tokyo). Like the obligation of military service, this was a reflection of traditional feudal practice. By the end of the sixteenth century most daimyo required their vassals to live in the castle town of their domain. Many also kept the wives, heirs, or principal retainers of their allies as hostages in order to secure their loyalty. Hideyoshi had done so himself. Both these practices were combined by Ieyasu and his successors in the *sankin-kōtai*, or alternate attendance system. Following the battle of Sekigahara, many of the *tozama* daimyo had sent hostages to Edo, and either as a sign of their loyalty or out of a desire to be close to the center of power, had built large residences there for their wives and children. Expanding on this informal practice, the bakufu soon required all daimyo, whatever their size or status, to build mansions in the capital to house their families and a suitable retinue of attendants. Although his family was obliged to remain in Edo, the daimyo himself was required only to alternate his residence each year between the capital and the domain headquarters. In 1635 the bakufu issued elaborate laws regulating this system of alternate attendance, which kept the entire daimyo class under surveillance and made Edo the castle town of the whole country.

Like the sixteenth-century daimyo, the bakufu had its own house code. In 1615 it issued the Laws Governing Military Houses (Buke Shohatto), which applied both to the daimyo and the warrior class as a whole. In part this fundamental document was simply a guide for the conduct of the warrior class, urging them to pursue the arts of war and the arts of peace, to avoid immoral or disorderly conduct, and to exercise frugality. But it also established regulations designed to prevent the recurrence of political disorder and anarchy. The daimyo were enjoined not to harbor those who broke laws within their domains, to expel retainers who committed murder or treason, and to give no sanctuary to those who plotted rebellion. Moreover, if a daimyo knew of seditious activities on a neighboring domain, he was admonished to make this known to bakufu authorities. The daimyo were forbidden to build new castles, to repair military fortifications, or to contract marriages with other daimyo families without bakufu permission. Like the rest of the bakufu system, these laws were permeated with a profound distrust of the daimyo and a fear that rebellion lay close beneath the surface of Tokugawa hegemony.

In its origins, the Edo bakufu was shaped by an attempt to control the daimyo through the systematic imposition of feudal practices from above. Like the sixteenth-century daimyo, it used feudal ties as a means of establishing political and military control over the country. But with the passage of time, many of these feudal forms were interpreted in a new way. By the latter half of the seventeenth century, the shogun was thought of less as a feudal overlord than as a territorial ruler with public responsibilities. Under the influence of the Confucian political thought promoted by Ieyasu and his successors, there developed the theory that the emperor delegated to the shogun the power to preserve the peace of the realm and to prevent misgovernment. According to this theory of delegation, the shogun in turn entrusted many powers to the daimyo, who ruled their domains with his consent. As the shogun came to be thought of as the loyal official of the emperor, so the daimyo were regarded as the loyal officials of the shogun. This theory was perhaps inaccurate as a historical description of how political authority had evolved in Japan, but it was increasingly accurate as a description of the way the country was actually governed. During the seventeenth century, beneath the façade of feudal forms, the country was moving more and more in the direction of decentralized bureaucratic government.

THE GROWTH
OF
BUREAUCRACY

In shaping a new political system on the experience of local daimyo government, the bakufu never attempted to exercise all the powers normally associated with full sovereignty. Unlike the postfeudal monarchies of Western Europe, the bakufu never imposed a national system of taxation, raised no mercenary or conscript army, or even attempted to establish a truly national system of law. The individual domain was highly autonomous in its internal affairs. In the administration of justice, for example, the writ of the bakufu ran only within its own direct domains and regulated only its direct vassals. The laws of the bakufu applied to the daimyo, but not to the population of their domains. The right to adjudicate civil disputes was normally vested in the holder of the land, whether he was a daimyo or a minor vassal of the bakufu. Even in criminal cases, which we usually regard as the concern of the state rather than private individuals, the daimyo had full power to arrest, judge, and punish offenders so long as the parties involved were registered residents of his domain and so long as the laws of the daimyo were administered in conformity with those of the bakufu. The bakufu courts could intervene only in civil or criminal cases involving residents of two different domains.

In actual practice, local administration was shared by both the bakufu and the daimyo. Each domain, including the bakufu's own direct holdings, was administered as an independent unit with its own officials and its own regulations. There was much uniformity in local administrative practices; in many ways, just as the bakufu was a daimyo domain writ large, each domain was a bakufu writ small. In 1615 the bakufu declared that "in all matters the example set by Edo is to be followed in all provinces and places." Many of the daimyo followed this injunction since they had risen from the original vassal band of the Tokugawa family. Others did so partly because the bakufu encouraged such imitation and partly because they constantly had the example of the bakufu before them during their regular attendance at the capital. The pressures toward conformity were, on the whole, stronger than the desire for innovation.

The separate administrative responsibilities of the bakufu and the daimyo militated against bakufu interference in the internal affairs of the domains. In England and France royal judges slowly but surely extended the authority of the monarch at the expense of feudal prerogatives, but in Japan the bakufu contented itself with a supervisory function. It maintained four or five inspectors-general, called *ōmetsuke*, who were charged with making sure that the daimyo observed its regulations. Similarly, from the reign of Iemitsu, the bakufu dispatched auditing officials (*junkenshi*) to investigate the wealth of the domains, their administration and finances, military strength, and size of their populations. All this circumscribed the powers of the daimyo, but it left administrative autonomy in his hands. For the people on the domains, it was the daimyo's officials rather than those of the bakufu with whom they dealt in their daily lives.

The division of the country into so many autonomous or semiautonomous political units was accompanied by a proliferation of bureaucratic posts. By the end of the seventeenth century, Japan was probably one of the most thoroughly governed countries in the world. The bakufu had an administrative hierarchy of over 17,000 civil and military officials, and the daimyo had similar administrative staffs of their own. In recruiting men for these great bureaucratic establishments, both the bakufu and the daimyo drew on their own retainers. In the case of the bakufu, the shogun recruited his highest advisers and counselors from the ranks of the *fudai* daimyo, while the lesser of his direct vassals, the *hatamoto* ("bannermen") and the *gokenin*, served in less important posts. The less trustworthy *tozama* daimyo were naturally excluded from positions of responsibility within the bakufu, as were the related daimyo, who could exert only unofficial influence.

A similar situation prevailed in the local domains. The more important vassals assisted the daimyo in making domain policy, while others served as magistrates and judges, superintendents of finance, administrators of the castle town, and even in lowly positions like clerks, tax collectors, record keepers, or storehouse attendants. With few exceptions, such as village headmen or certain privileged merchants charged with financial duties, positions of administrative and political responsibility were limited to members of the warrior class. In contrast to Europe, where the postfeudal monarchs recruited their royal officials from the Church, the universities, the bourgeoisie, and the smaller and needier members of the feudal aristocracy, Japan had no body of professional administrators dependent on a sovereign for their authority and income. The growth of a bureaucracy was not a challenge to the old feudal class, but rather an outgrowth of its authority.

The conversion of the warrior class from fighting men into civil officials was in large measure the consequence of the peace that followed the establishment of the Edo bakufu. There were no major disturbances in the country after the Shimabara revolt of 1637–1638. In 1649 the bakufu issued regulations severely limiting the number of retainers a daimyo could keep in training and ready for combat. By 1700 military duties were limited to a small number of families that held hereditary membership in the domain forces. The majority of the warrior class were thus robbed of their old function in society. But since they were still maintained economically by the daimyo, it was more practical and less expensive to press them into service as civil officials than to recruit members from other classes in society. Military ranks were still assigned to warriors, but in practice such ranks were made a qualification for bureaucratic posts rather than military posts. The writing brush therefore began to replace the sword as the primary tool of the warrior's trade.

This transformation of the warrior class from fighting men into civil officials was also facilitated by their changing economic relationship to the daimyo. Although most warriors had moved from the land into the castle towns of their daimyo by the beginning of the seventeenth century, there were two main ways in which they were granted incomes. Some retainers, usually the less powerful ones, received stipends in rice directly from the daimyo's granaries. Others held fiefs, from which they collected their own taxes or rents, whose peasant labor they could conscript, and over whose inhabitants they exercised judicial powers. In contrast to the stipended retainers, the fief holders were richer and more powerful, often being the descendants of petty lords or castellans whom the daimyo's ancestors had brought under control in the course of unifying his domain.

During the seventeenth century, most daimyo, in order to consolidate control over their domains, attempted to convert fief holders into stipend holders by slowly reducing their powers over the fiefs or by commuting the fiefs directly into stipends. They did this primarily to increase their own tax revenues rather than to reduce the political strength of their retainers. By 1700 or so, perhaps 90 percent of the daimyo had converted their fief holders into stipendiaries. In contrast to the previous century, when the typical warrior lived close to the land and dominated the peasantry directly, the typical warrior of the late seventeenth century was a resident of a castle town living off income granted him at the daimyo's discretion. One contemporary observer pointed out that the warriors were "living as in an inn," cut off from the land that was originally their main source of strength and with all their economic wants provided for them by their master. The size of their stipend could be increased, decreased, and even taken away—all at the pleasure of the daimyo. The individual warrior was thus far weaker and less independent than ever before in the history of the class.

The new social and political role of the warrior had important effects on the concept of feudal loyalty. The relationship between lord and vassal was no longer as mutual as it had been in the era of feudal anarchy. Since the daimyo could increase, decrease, or take away a retainer's stipend, the tie between the lord and vassal became one-sided. The lord no longer needed his vassals as fighting men, but they continued to need him as a source of their wealth and income. At the same time, the bond between the daimyo and his retainers was much less personal than the primitive vassalage tie. Loyalty was automatic, not voluntary. The warrior swore an oath of allegiance to his daimyo regardless of whether his lord was personally weak or strong, benevolent or tyrannical, warm and compassionate or cold and aloof. The pledge of loyalty became a ritual act, performed by the warrior because he had inherited the obligation of loyalty from his father. The daimyo was less a personal leader than the head of a bureaucratic hierarchy to which the warrior belonged. One historian has suggested that the loyalty of the warrior class in Tokugawa times was as much directed toward the domain as it was toward the daimyo, who symbolized its unity. Such loyalty was perhaps more akin to patriotism than to the emotional bonds of the pre-Kamakura warrior bands.

Equally interesting, the values of the warrior seem likewise to have undergone a change. To be sure, the young warrior was still "educated for death." From an early age he was taught the use of the sword, was instilled with the importance of family honor, and was expected to submit unconditionally to the commands of his superiors. He was also inculcated with the importance of courage, bravado, and dauntlessness. But it became equally important for him to learn to read and write and to practice the virtues of self-control, frugality, and hard work. In a society where he had to serve as an honest and industrious official, these values were far more essential than those that might help him survive on the battlefield.

The warrior of the late seventeenth century was a far different type from his passionate, violent, and often ostentatious ancestors. Self-controlled, abstemious, and hard-working, he was less a man in constant readiness for war than one in search of a personal equilibrium necessary to succeed in a highly controlled bureaucratic society. Although he was still taught that he should be ready to die for his lord on the battlefield, the chances of having to do so were slim indeed. Obedience to the lord was defined far more frequently in terms of public service, as was the social role of the warrior. According to one late seventeenth-century writer, the warrior stood above the rest of the population not because he was a fighting man, but because "he leads a virtuous life, cultivates and brings peace to the world by governing the country." This pacific ideal was surely a far cry from the warrior heroes portrayed in the military romances of earlier centuries, who were feted for their boldness, vigor, and military prowess rather than for the moral example they set for the common people.

THE FREEZING OF SOCIETY

The bureaucratization of the warrior class was accompanied by their conversion into a legally privileged class. Throughout its first century the bakufu attempted to divide society into clearly defined status groups set apart by law and custom. In their pursuit of order, the men of the early seventeenth century looked back with distaste on the social fluidity of the "warring states" period, when vassals had overturned their lords and peasants had become warriors. They were anxious to perpetuate the principle that "Lord and vassal, superior and inferior, should observe what is proper to their station in life." Although such a principle operated within the warrior class through the maintenance of hereditary military ranks, it was meant to apply to the rest of the population as well. The bakufu was particularly concerned to maintain a clear social distinction between the rulers and the ruled. In concrete terms, this meant maintaining the warriors as a hereditary ruling class clearly distinct from peasants and townsmen.

The policy of dividing the population into commoners and warriors was not a new one, but had its beginnings in the attempt of the sixteenth-century daimyo to separate those who were obligated to provide military service from those obligated to pay taxes. Both Nobunaga and Hideyoshi had continued this practice of setting the fighting men apart from the rest of society in hopes of ending local disorder.

In part they had done so through the disarming of the peasantry and the other commoners. Following a practice begun by Nobunaga in 1576 and 1578, Hideyoshi conducted a series of "sword hunts" in the 1580s aimed at taking weapons and arms out of the hands of the farmers and townsmen. The disarming of the nonwarriors was accompanied by the carrying out of nationwide land surveys. The registers produced by these surveys designated as peasantry those who occupied the land and were obliged to pay taxes, and set them apart from those designated as warriors, who held fiefs or stipends and were responsible for military service. The separation of warrior from commoner received further impetus from Hideyoshi after he had virtually completed military unification of the country. In 1590 he issued his famous Three-article Edict, which prohibited former warriors from moving into peasant villages, restricted peasants to agriculture and forbade them from entering trade or commerce, and prohibited the warriors from changing lords. Warrior, peasant, and townsman—each had his separate status and fixed place in the social structure.

The freezing of society that had begun before 1600 was accelerated with the onset of peace and the decline of opportunities for mobility. The separation of classes, already firmly established by the beginning of the century, was reinforced by the laws of both the bakufu and the individual daimyo. The warrior class alone had the privilege of bearing surnames and carrying the two swords that were the principal mark of the class. Occasionally, a townsman or a peasant might be allowed to take a surname, or perhaps even carry a short sword, but this was done only with special permission. The bakufu also attempted to maintain the distinction between the different orders of society by issuing sumptuary regulations specifying the style of clothing, size of house, habits of consumption, and even forms of entertainment appropriate to each order. Such regulations increased from the middle of the seventeenth century.

The penal laws of the bakufu also clearly set the

rulers apart from the ruled. Warriors were not punished for the same crimes as the commoners. A warrior might not be punished for cutting down a peasant who was insolent or truculent toward him, but a peasant who killed his neighbor for the same reason would be guilty of murder. By the same token, a warrior who indulged in gambling or robbery would be punished far more severely than a commoner because he was held to have higher standards of personal behavior. Similarly, the warrior was rarely subject to the same degrading punishments as the commoner, since the honor of the whole class had to be protected.

By the middle of the seventeenth century it had become common to justify this status-divided society by a theory of social utility borrowed from Confucianism. In the Confucian vision of society, all people could be divided into four classes—officials, peasants, artisans, and merchants. Each class was given precedence according to the usefulness of its role in society. Officials, which in Japan were equated with the warrior class, were the most important because they maintained the social order that permitted the rest of society to live and go about its business in peace. Peasants were next in importance, for by their labor the other members of society were fed. Artisans and merchants, who made up the townsman class, performed less essential roles. The artisan produced goods, but often these were unnecessary or luxury items, and the merchants merely carried goods from places where they were plentiful to places where they were scarce. Like the theory of delegation that had come to justify the political order, this theory of social utility held that the hierarchy of the four classes was an inviolable one. The social order and the political system were not the creation of men but part of the natural order of the universe, and any attempt to alter human society would upset this order.

On the whole, this unegalitarian social ethic was rarely challenged. To be sure, a warrior family might adopt a merchant's son as an heir, or a poor warrior might abandon his status and his stipend to become an artisan or a handicraft worker—but such mobility between social orders was rare and without official sanction. By the late seventeenth century, most men remained in the social order in which they were born, and rarely were they, or their sons, able to leave it. What social mobility that did occur usually took place within one of the major classes. A poor tenant might become a rich landlord, a peddler might make himself into a shopkeeper or even a well-to-do wholesale merchant, or a low-ranking samurai might rise relatively high in the administrative hierarchy of his domain. But on the whole most men accepted their station in life.

This social stability was all the more remarkable since it was maintained in the face of vigorous commercial development. The reconstruction of the country after a century of war, a burst of population growth, and the establishment of some degree of political unity had brought about an economic boom. By 1700, this prosperity had produced a class of wealthy merchants in the two great urban centers of Osaka and Edo. Many of the merchants had even become the creditors of the daimyo and of the bakufu itself, which borrowed from them to finance an increasingly luxurious style of life. Despite their considerable economic power, the merchant class acquired neither political power nor social status comparable to that of the warrior class. In contrast to many parts of Western Europe, where mercantile towns bought charters of self-government from the monarchs or the feudal magnates, Japan's large cities remained under the control of the bakufu, and the provincial castle towns, which served as local economic centers, were still controlled by the daimyo.

Neither the bakufu nor the local domain governments attempted to establish regular taxes on domestic trade. In accordance with Confucian economic ideas, they felt that taxes on commerce would only drive up prices and that agriculture should be the main source of revenue. As a result, the merchant classes were deprived of much of the political leverage that their counterparts in Europe enjoyed as a result of monarchs or local lords seeking new sources of revenue in commerce. In any case, the outlook of Japanese merchants was far more docile. There is every evidence that the merchant princes of Osaka and Edo accepted the Confucian ethics promoted by the bakufu and that they realized their business activities rested largely on the tolerance of the political authorities. The relation between the merchants and the political authorities was therefore one of symbiosis rather than competition.

By 1700, in contrast to the more dynamic post-feudal Europe, political change in Japan had come to a standstill. Although some minor institutional change took place, the general outline of the political system, which preserved the forms if not the functions of feudal government, remained unchallenged. The probability of change from within was slight indeed. The bakufu's system of political controls allowed the daimyo few opportunities for revolt; the grant of guaranteed incomes to the warrior class kept them content, on the whole; and the continuing dependence of the bakufu and the daimyo on agricultural rather than commercial revenues minimized the potential influence of the merchant class.

Nor were there pressures for change from without. The Chinese, unified under the Ch'ing dynasty in 1644, were more concerned with subduing the peoples of central and inner Asia than with expeditions against her maritime neighbors. Similarly, the Europeans, who had first reached the shores of Japan in the early sixteenth century, took little interest in so remote, isolated, and militarily advanced a country as Japan. They turned their energies instead toward South Asia, the East Indies, and the New World, the richness of whose resources made conquest attractive and the weakness of whose peoples made conquest easy. Finally, the bakufu, which had learned of Spanish encroachments in the Philippines, decided to close off contact with the outside world for fear that those few missionaries and traders who did reach Japan might be the vanguard of military invaders. As foreigners were kept out, so the Japanese were kept in, and Japanese efforts at overseas trade and exploration, which had begun briefly in the sixteenth century, came to an abrupt end.

THE
ABOLITION
OF FEUDAL
FORMS

Effective political controls, social inertia, and isolation kept Japan's peculiar postfeudal settlement intact for nearly two and a half centuries. It was only under pressure from the outside that it finally collapsed. From the beginning of the nineteenth century, as the Americans, the English, and the Russians began to show interest in developing trade with the countries of East Asia, sporadic attempts were made to breach Japan's seclusion. None succeeded until the arrival of Admiral Perry in 1853. His adamant demands that Japan be opened to commerce and normal diplomatic relations with the outside world provoked a major national crisis. In the decade that followed, the government at Edo, militarily powerless in face of gunboat diplomacy, was forced to sign a series of "unequal treaties" that opened certain ports to foreign trade and gave the foreigners extraterritorial privileges. As a result, its prestige declined rapidly. The bakufu's failure to meet the challenge of the nineteenth century revived the long-slumbering hostilities of the seventeenth, provoking exactly the kind of daimyo revolt that Ieyasu and his heirs had feared.

In 1868 an alliance of powerful *tozama* domains, led by Satsuma and Chōshū, carried out a coup d'état that restored sovereign control to the emperor. Although it toppled the bakufu, this event, known as the Meiji Restoration, was neither antifeudal in inspiration nor popular in character. The men who carried out the Restoration were interested in protecting the country against further Western encroachment; they had no interest in destroying the fabric of the old society. Indeed, the new imperial government at first even continued to use the administrative structure of the daimyo domains to govern the country and made every effort to provide for daimyo participation in important government decisions.

Within a year or two of the Restoration, however, it became clear that the country could not afford to preserve the remnants of feudal government if it were to survive in the modern world. For one thing, it was impossible for Japan to deal with the Western powers as a united nation if it remained a conglomeration of disjointed local daimyo domains. Even the last shogun, Tokugawa Keiki, declared in his abdication, "Now that foreign intercourse becomes daily more extensive, the foundations of government will collapse unless administration is directed from one central point." It was also clear that the preservation of old political forms would be costly and inefficient. Much of the government's budget, for example, was consumed by the payments of rice stipends to the members of the warrior class, many of whom performed no official function or service. Finally, the Western nations continually pressed the imperial government to establish a modern political and legal system as a condition for renegotiating the "unequal treaties."

During the early 1870s the government therefore began to abolish remaining feudal forms in the name of building national strength. The old system of social classes was eliminated in order to make all subjects of the emperor equal before the law. Peasants were given the right to own land, and former warriors to engage in any profession they might choose. The old administrative structure was dismantled as well. The daimyo domains were gradually deprived of their autonomy, and by 1871 they had been replaced by a system of prefectures governed by centrally appointed officials. Finally, and most significantly, the special position of the warrior class came under attack. Members of the class were systematically stripped of their officially guaranteed stipends and income, and the establishment of a universal military conscription system in 1873 finally eliminated the raison d'être for a specially privileged class of fighting men. With the promulgation in 1876 of an edict that forbade private citizens from wearing the two swords that set the warrior apart from the common people, the last vestiges of the feudal order came to an end.

The process of political modernization occurred far more rapidly in Japan than in Western Europe, where it was carried out not only much more slowly, but much more painfully, and with much less sense of urgency. In the space of a decade, the Japanese experienced a political change that had taken centuries in some parts of the West. The British minister in Japan at the time remarked that in Europe a reform as momentous as the abolition of the daimyo domains could have been accomplished only after several years of warfare, and he could regard it only as an act of providence that it succeeded in Japan with the simple issuance of an edict. To be sure, the dismantling of the old order did rouse some resistance. There were sporadic revolts carried out by former warriors in the 1870s, culminating in the great rebellion of 1877 led by Saigo Takamori, one of the original leaders of the Meiji Restoration. But most of these revolts were highly local in character and relatively small in scale.

How can one account for the ease with which feudal privileges were eliminated? In part, of course, the new government succeeded in building up an army and a police force that was able to keep political disorder under control. It also made a generous financial settlement with the daimyo and their vassals, whose annual stipends were commuted into cash payments or government bonds. Many members of the former warrior class used these funds as capital to found businesses and participate in the industrialization of the economy promoted by the government. At the same time, many former warriors were absorbed into the new structure of government as minor officials, army officers, policemen, and schoolteachers. Their bureaucratic education had prepared them for such occupations and enabled them to find useful work despite the elimination of their old privileges. Indeed, for many of the lower ranking members of the warrior class, the abolition of the old social distinctions opened new opportunities to rise in the world. Though the Restoration had robbed them of their special position in society, it had liberated them as well.

But perhaps the fundamental reason why the new

government met with such little resistance was that the remaining forms of feudalism had long since lost their original function. It was over two and a half centuries since the warriors had followed their daimyo to the battlefield, and the social and political practices that originally developed to keep them in a state of readiness no longer had any meaning. The Restoration had not struck down a vigorous feudal government, but one that had already been embalmed by the Tokugawa. It is not surprising that it showed so little will to resist.

Bibliography

Students interested in the study of Japanese feudalism will find several works of indispensable value. For those unacquainted with premodern Japanese history, an excellent introduction is George B. Sansom's highly readable *Japan: A Short Cultural History* (2nd rev. ed.; New York: Appleton-Century-Crofts, 1952). A masterful survey of the institutional development of premodern Japan is to be found in John Whitney Hall, *Government and Local Power in Japan, 500 to 1700: A Study Based on Bizen Province* (Princeton, N.J.: Princeton University Press, 1966). A valuable general essay on institutional developments, together with translated documents illustrating the workings of Japanese feudal institutions, may be found in the pioneering work by Kan'ichi Asakawa, *The Documents of Iriki* (Tokyo: Japan Society for the Promotion of Science, 1955). A collection of other essays by Asakawa is *Land and Society in Medieval Japan* (Tokyo: Japan Society for the Promotion of Science, 1965). The only systematic attempt at a comparison of medieval Japanese and European institutions may be found in Frédéric Joüon des Longrais, *L'est et l'ouest: institutions du Japon et de l'occident comparée* (Paris and Tokyo: Maison Franco-Japonaise, 1958). All these works deal with the entire period covered in this book. More specialized or detailed historical works are listed below.

Chapter 1: What Is Feudalism?

* Bloch, Marc. *Feudal Society*. Chicago: University of Chicago Press, 1961.

Calmette, Joseph. *La Société Féodale*. Paris: Librairie Armand Colin, 1947.

Coulbourn, Rushton (ed.). *Feudalism in History*. Princeton, N.J.: Princeton University Press, 1956.

---

* Available in paperback.

Ganshof, F. L. *Feudalism*. London: Longmans, Green, 1951.

Hall, John Whitney. "Feudalism in Japan—A Reassessment," *Comparative Studies in History and Society*, Vol. V (October 1962), pp. 15–51.

* Stephenson, Carl. *Medieval Feudalism*. Ithaca, N.Y.: Cornell University Press, 1942.

* ———. *Medieval Institutions*. Ithaca, N.Y.: Cornell University Press, 1954.

———. "The Origin and Significance of Feudalism," *American Historical Review*, Vol. XLVI (July 1941), pp. 788–812.

* Strayer, Joseph R. *Feudalism*. Princeton, N.J.: Van Nostrand, 1965.

Chapter 2: From Tribal Rule to Civil Monarchy

Asakawa, Kan'ichi. "The Life of a Monastic Shō in Medieval Japan," *Annual Report of the American Historical Association*, Vol. I (1919), pp. 311–42.

Aston, W. G. *Nihongi: Chronicles of Japan from Earliest Times to A.D. 696*. London: Kegan Paul, 1896.

Kidder, J. Edward. *Japan Before Buddhism*. New York: Praeger, 1959.

Morris, Ivan. *The World of the Shining Prince: Court Life in Ancient Japan*. New York: Knopf, 1964.

Reischauer, Robert K. *Early Japanese History*. Part A. Princeton, N.J.: Princeton University Press, 1937.

Sansom, George B. "Early Japanese Law and Administration," *Transactions of the Asiatic Society of Japan*, Second Series, Vol. IX (1932), pp. 67–109; XI (1934), pp. 117–49.

———. *History of Japan to 1334*. Stanford, Calif.: Stanford University Press, 1958.

Tsunoda, Ryusaku, and L. Carrington Goodrich. *Japan in the Chinese Dynastic Histories*. Pasadena, Calif.: P. D. and Ione Perkins, 1951.

Chapter 3: From Civil Monarchy to Warrior Rule

Asakawa, Kan'ichi. "Some Aspects of Japanese Feudal Institutions," *Transactions of the Asiatic Society of Japan*, First Series, Vol. XLVI (1918), pp. 76–102.

———. "The Founding of the Shogunate by Minamoto Yoritomo," *Seminarium Kondakovianum*, Vol. VI (1933), pp. 109–29.

Hall, John Carey. "Japanese Feudal Laws: The Institutes of Judicature, being a translation of Go Seibai Shikimoku; The Magisterial Code of the Hōjō Power-Holders (1232)," *Transactions of the Asiatic Society of Japan*, First Series, Vol. XXXIV (1906), pp. 1–44.

Joün des Longrais, Frédéric. *Age de Kamakura, sources (1180–1333), archives, chartes japonaises (monjo)*. Paris and Tokyo: Maison Franco-Japonaise, 1950.

Kellogg, E. R. (tr.). "Hogen Monogatari," *Transactions of the Asiatic Society of Japan*, Vol. XL (1917), pp. 25–117.

McCullough, Helen Craig (tr.). "A Tale of Mutsu," *Harvard Journal of Asiatic Studies*, Vol. XXV (1964–1965), pp. 178–211.

Sadler, Arthur Lindsay (tr.). "Heike Monogatari," *Transactions of the Asiatic Society of Japan*, First Series, Vol. XLVI (1918), pp. i–xiv, 1–278; XLIX (1921), pp. i–ii, 1–354.

Shinoda, Minoru. *The Founding of the Kamakura Shogunate, 1180–1185*. New York: Columbia University Press, 1960.

Chapter 4:   From Warrior Rule to Feudal Anarchy

Hall, John Carey. "Japanese Feudal Laws: The Ashikaga Code," *Transactions of the Asiatic Society of Japan*, First Series, Vol. XXXVI (1908), pp. 3–25.

Hall, John Whitney. "The Castle Town and Japan's Modern Urbanization," *Far Eastern Quarterly*, Vol. XV (November 1955), pp. 37–56.

————. "Foundations of the Modern Japanese Daimyo," *The Journal of Asian Studies*, Vol. XX (May 1961), pp. 317–29.

Ishii, Ryōsuke. "On Japanese Possession of Real Property— A Study of *chigyō* in the Middle Ages," *Japan Annual of Law and Politics*, No. 1 (1952), pp. 149–62.

McCullough, Helen Craig (tr.). *The Taiheiki, A Chronicle of Medieval Japan*. New York: Columbia University Press, 1959.

Sansom, George B. *A History of Japan, 1334–1615*. Stanford, Calif.: Stanford University Press, 1961.

Varley, Paul. *The Ōnin War*. New York: Columbia University Press, 1967.

Chapter 5:   From Feudal Anarchy to National Unity

Bellah, Robert N. *Tokugawa Religion: The Values of Pre-industrial Japan.* New York: Free Press, 1957.

Craig, Albert. *Chōshū in the Meiji Restoration.* Cambridge, Mass.: Harvard University Press, 1961.

Crawcour, E. S. "Changes in Japanese Commerce in the Tokugawa Period," *The Journal of Asian Studies,* Vol. XXII (August 1963), pp. 387–400.

Dore, Ronald P. *Education in Tokugawa Japan.* Berkeley, Calif.: University of California Press, 1965.

Earl, David N. *Emperor and Nation in Japan.* Seattle, Wash.: University of Washington Press, 1964.

Hall, John Carey. "Japanese Feudal Laws, III: The Tokugawa Legislation, Parts I–III," *Transactions of the Asiatic Society of Japan,* First Series, Vol. XXXVIII (1911), pp. 269–331.

————. "The Tokugawa Legislation, IV," *Transactions of the Asiatic Society of Japan,* First Series, Vol. XLI (1913), pp. 683–804.

Hall, John W., and Marius B. Jansen (ed.). *Studies in the Institutional History of Early Modern Japan.* Princeton, N.J.: Princeton University Press, 1968.

Henderson, Dan F. *Conciliation and Japanese Law: Tokugawa and Modern.* Vol. I. Seattle, Wash.: University of Washington Press, 1965.

Sadler, Arthur Lindsay. *The Maker of Modern Japan: The Life of Tokugawa Ieyasu (1542–1616).* London: Allen and Unwin, 1937.

Sansom, George B. *A History of Japan, 1615–1867.* Stanford, Calif.: Stanford University Press, 1963.

Sheldon, Charles D. *The Rise of the Merchant Class in Tokugawa Japan, 1600–1868: An Introductory Survey.* Locust Valley, N.Y.: J. J. Augustin, 1958.

Totman, Conrad. *Politics in the Tokugawa Bakufu, 1600–1843.* Cambridge, Mass.: Harvard University Press, 1967.

Tsukahira, Toshio. *Feudal Control in Tokugawa Japan: The Sankin Kōtai System.* Cambridge, Mass.: Harvard University Press, 1966.

Chronology

late 3rd–early 4th centuries	Establishment of the Yamato state
early 7th–early 8th centuries	Importation of Chinese political ideas and institutions
645–646	Promulgation of Taika reforms
702	Completion of Taihō Code
710	Permanent capital established at Nara
718	Completion of Yōrō Code
794	Capital moved to Heian (Kyoto)
early 10th century	Political emergence of warrior chieftains
939–940	Revolt of Taira Masakado
1051–1062	Early Nine Years War
1083–1087	Later Three Years War
1156–1180	Domination of court by Taira Kiyomori
1180–1185	Gempei War (collapse of Taira) and establishment of Kamakura bakufu
1192	Minamoto Yoritomo appointed shogun
1221	Shōkyū War
1232	Promulgation of Jōei Formulary
1274, 1281	Mongol invasions
1334	Fall of Kamakura bakufu
1336–1392	War between Northern and Southern courts
1338	Ashikaga Takauji appointed shogun
1467–1477	Ōnin War
mid-15th–mid-16th centuries	"Warring states" period and rise of daimyo
1542	Arrival of Portuguese
1560–1590	Military reunification
1568	Kyoto occupied by Oda Nobunaga
1573	Fall of Muromachi bakufu
1580s	Hideyoshi's "sword hunts"
1582	Assassination of Nobunaga
1592–1593, 1597–1598	Hideyoshi's expeditions against Korea

1595	Hideyoshi's national land survey
early 17th century	Political unification and establishment of Edo bakufu
1600	Battle of Sekigahara
1603	Tokugawa Ieyasu appointed shogun
1615	Promulgation of Laws Governing Military Houses
1635, 1642	Promulgation of *sankin-kōtai* regulations
1636–1641	Establishment of seclusion policy
1853	Arrival of Admiral Perry
1867–1868	Fall of Edo bakufu and restoration of Imperial rule
1871	Abolition of daimyo domains
1873	Creation of a conscript army
1876	Prohibition on wearing of swords

Glossary

Amaterasu	Sun goddess, ancestress of the imperial family.
ashigaru	Foot soldier.
Ashikaga	Dynasty of shoguns under the Muromachi bakufu.
bakufu	Warrior government headed by shogun.
be	Group of hereditary serfs engaged in the same occupation.
Buke Shohatto	Regulations governing the daimyo and direct retainers of the Edo bakufu.
bushi	General term for mounted warrior.
bushi no tōryō	Chieftain of a regional warrior band.
chigyō	Possession of land through occupancy.
daimyō	Feudal lord.
fudai	Hereditary vassal; under the Edo bakufu, the vassal daimyo.
Fujiwara	Aristocratic family which dominated the imperial court from the mid-ninth to the mid-eleventh centuries.
gekokujo	Betrayal of a lord by his vassal.
Gempei War	War between the Minamoto and the Taira (1180–1185).
gokenin	"Honorable houseman": under the Kamakura bakufu, the direct vassals of the bakufu; under the Edo bakufu, the smaller direct vassals of the bakufu, usually with incomes of less than 100 koku of rice.
hanzei	Foraging tax.
hatamoto	The larger direct vassals of the Edo bakufu, usually with incomes of 100 to 10,000 koku of rice.
Hōjō	Warrior family which dominated the Kamakura bakufu.
jitō	Land stewards placed on private estates (*shōen*).
Jōei Formulary	Basic law code of the Kamakura bakufu.
kashin	Vassal or retainer.
kenin	Vassal or retainer.
koku	Unit of measure equal to about five bushels.
Minamoto	Family of warrior chieftains, rivals of the Taira.
samurai	Warrior; strictly speaking, a mounted warrior with retainers.
sankin-kōtai	Alternate attendance of daimyo at the shogun's court in Edo.

shiki	Rights to income from land on private estates (*shōen*).
shimpan	Related daimyo of the Tokugawa family.
Shintō	The indigenous religion of the Japanese.
shōen	Private estate exempt from taxation and administrative interference by the imperial government.
shōgun	Warrior monarch who headed the bakufu.
shugo	Provincial constable, first appointed by Yoritomo.
Taihō Code	Legal and administrative code based on the Chinese model issued in 702.
Taira	Family of warrior chieftains, rivals of the Minamoto.
tennō	Emperor or civil monarch.
Tokugawa	Dynasty of shoguns under the Edo bakufu.
tozama	Ally; under the Edo bakufu, the allied daimyo of the Tokugawa family.
Yōrō Code	Legal and administrative code based on the Chinese model issued in 718.
za	Monopoly association of merchants or artisans.

Index

Abe family, 41
Agriculture, 9, 16–17, 34
Alternate attendance system (*sankin kōtai*), 92
Amaterasu, 18
Ashigaru, 74
Ashikaga family, 66
Ashikaga Takauji, 61, 65
Ashikaga Yoshiaki, 83
Ashikaga, Yoshimasa, 68

Bakufu, *see* Monarchy, warrior
Be, 16
Buddhism, 21
Buke Shohatto, 92–93
Bureaucratic government, 7, 14
   under legal codes, 22–23, 26–27
   in China, 25–26
   decline of, 27–28, 31
   in Edo period, 95–96
Bushi no tōryo, 44–46, 71

Carolingian empire, 35, 56, 66
Castles, 75
Central Asia, 25
   influence on Japan, 14–15
Charlemagne, 56
Chigyō, 71–72
China
   bureaucratic government in, 7, 25–26
   influence on Japan, 13, 20–26, 82
Chōshū, 104
Civil disorder, 35–36, 43–45, 57–58, 67–69
   See also Civil war; Gempei War; Ōnin War;
     Shōkyū War; "Warring states" period
Civil war, 61–62, 63, 66, 68
Clan system, 15–16, 25

Confucianism
    political ideas of, 21, 93
    social ethic of, 101, 103
    economic theory of, 102
Court aristocracy, 34
    growth of, 25–29
    and estate system, 29
    and warrior class, 45–47, 62–64
    decline of, 68–69

Daimyo, 69
    origins of, 69–70
    domains of, 75–76
    vassal bands of, 70–71
    contributions to reunification, 82, 87–88
    under Edo bakufu, 88–93
    See also Fudai daimyo; Shimpan
        daimyo; Tozama daimyo

Edo bakufu
    establishment of, 86–88
    character of, 87–88
    policy toward daimyo, 89–93
    policy of social stratification, 99–100
    stability of, 103–04
    fall of, 104
Emperor, *see* Monarchy, civil
Estates, private (*shōen*)
    origins of, 29–31
    description of, 31–32
    land holding on, 32–33
    and local warriors, 37, 62–64
    protected by bakufu, 51–52
    expropriation of, 62–64
Examination system, government, 25–26

Feudal fees, 79–80
Feudalism
    problem of defining, 1–4, 11
    uses of term, 4–7
    characteristics of European, 7–11
    comparative study of, 7, 10–12

Feudalism (*continued*)
emergence of Japanese, 35–36, 57–58
end of European, 81
"centralized," 81–82
end of Japanese, 104–07
Feudal lord, *see Daimyo*
Fiefs
defined, 8
and manorial system, 9
and daimyo, 71–72
and vassalage under daimyo, 79–80
of the Edo period, 89–90
confiscation of daimyo, 89–90
conversion to stipends, 96–97
Firearms, 74–75, 84
Fudai daimyo, 88–89, 90, 91, 95
Fujiwara family, 27, 46
Fujiwara Sumitomo, 43

Gempei War, 48–49, 53, 68
Go-Daigo (Emperor), 60–61
Gokenin, 49–50, 51, 53–54, 55, 56, 59–60, 72
in Edo period, 95
Go-Toba (Emperor), 54

Hanzei, 63
Hatamoto, 95
Heian (Kyoto), as capital, 23
Hideyori, 86, 91
Hideyoshi, 83, 84–86, 87, 88, 99–100
Hōjō family, 53, 59, 61, 64
Hōjō Takatoki, 59
Hosokawa family, 68
House codes, 76

Inheritance practices, 17, 57–58, 67, 70

Jinshin disturbance, 26
Jitō, see Land stewards
Jōei Formulary, 55–56, 76
Junkenshi, 95

Kamakura bakufu
    establishment of, 48–49, 52
    change in leadership, 52–53
    compared with Carolingian empire, 56
    fall of, 58–61
Kantō plain, 37, 44, 48, 83, 86, 91
Kinship, role of, 8, 15, 18, 25, 39, 53–54
Kiyowara family, 41
Korea, 19, 86

Land-holding
    under legal codes, 23–24, 29–30
    on private estates, 32–33
    and warrior class, 37, 63–64
    under feudalism, 63–64, 66–67
    See also Chigyō; Shiki
Land stewards (*jitō*), 51–52, 54–55, 62–63
Law, idea of, 21–22
Legal codes, 21–22, 55–56, 76–77,
        92–93, 94, 100–01
    See also Buke Shohatto; House
        codes; Jōei Formulary
Local government and administration
    under legal codes, 24
    decline of, 28–29, 31, 54
    and warriors, 38–39
    under Kamakura bakufu, 50–52
    under Muromachi bakufu, 64–66
    under daimyo, 77–78
    under Edo bakufu, 94–95
Local warrior class
    origins of, 37
    before Kamakura period, 37–39
    land hunger of, 57–58
    during fourteenth and fifteenth centuries, 63–64
    separation from peasantry, 99–100
Loyalty, concept of
    before Kamakura period, 40
    early Kamakura period, 49–50, 53
    under daimyo, 71, 72–73
    in Edo period, 89, 97–98
Loyalty, oath of, 71, 89

Manorial system, 6, 9
  See also Estates, private
Meiji Restoration, 104–05, 107
Military organization
  under legal codes, 24–25, 36
  of pre-Kamakura warriors, 38–39, 43–44
  under daimyo, 72, 74
  under Edo bakufu, 91, 96
Military techniques, 15, 38, 42–43, 74
Minamoto family, 45–46, 47, 53
Minamoto Yoritomo, 48–52, 61, 65, 85, 87
Minamoto Yoshiie, 41–42
Minamoto Yoshitomo, 47
Monarchy, civil
  during Yamato period, 17–19
  conception of, 20–21
  changes in, 27–28
  residual authority of, 69, 82
  restoration of, 104
Monarchy, warrior, *see* Edo bakufu; Kamakura
  bakufu; Muromachi bakufu; *Shōgun*
Mongol invasions, 60
Multiple homages, 73
Muromachi bakufu
  establishment of, 61
  weaknesses of, 61, 64–65, 66, 68
  fall of, 83

Nara, as capital, 23
Nihongi, 17

Oda Nobunaga, 83–84, 86, 87, 88, 99–100
Ōmetsuke, 95
Ōnin War, 68–69, 88
Ōuchi family, 76

Peasantry, 16–17, 77–78
  separated from warriors, 99–100
Perry, Admiral, 104
Primogeniture, *see* Inheritance practices
Provincial constables (*shugo*), 50–51, 53,
  56, 63, 64–67, 69, 70

Saigo Takamori, 106

Samurai, *see* Local warrior class; Warrior bands; Warrior code; Warrior chieftains

Sankin kōta, 92

Satsuma, 104

Scutage, 79–80

Sekigahara, battle of, 87, 90

Shiki, 32–33, 50, 63, 65, 71

Shimabara revolt, 91, 96

Shimpan daimyo, 89, 90

Shintō, 18, 30

Shōen, see Estates, private

Shōgun, 52

Shōkyū War, 54–55

Shōtoku Taishi (Prince), 20, 25

Shugo, see Provincial constables

Social mobility, 70, 99, 101–02

Sui dynasty (China), 20

Taiheiki, 59

Taihō Code, 22

Taika coup d'etat, 26

Taira family, 45–46, 47

Taira Kiyomori, 47–48

Taira Masakado, 43

Taira Tadatsune, 43

Tale of Masakado, 40

Tale of Mutsu, 40, 41–42

T'ang dynasty (China), 20, 21, 22, 34

Taxation, 28
    under legal codes, 23–24, 29–31
    under Muromachi bakufu, 63
    under daimyo, 77

Tennō, see Monarchy, civil

Tokugawa Hidetada, 87

Tokugawa Iemitsu, 87

Tokugawa Ieyasu, 83, 86–88, 90, 91

Tokugawa Keiki, 105

Tozama daimyo, 88–89, 90, 91, 92, 95, 104

Trade and commerce, 9, 16, 76–77, 78–79, 101, 102

Vassalage
    defined, 8

Vassalage (*continued*)

    in pre-Kamakura warrior bands, 40

    under Yoritomo, 49–50, 52–53, 59

    "government by," 52, 56

    decline of, 59–60

    and provincial constables, 65–66

    and daimyo, 70–72, 73–74

Village, as administrative unit, 77

"Warring states" period, 69, 99

Warrior bands, 39–40, 43–44

Warrior code, 40–42, 98–99

Warrior chieftains (*bushi no tōryō*), 44–46, 71

Warriors, legal privileges of, 100–01, 105

Western expansion into East Asia, 103–04

Yamana family, 68

Yamato ruler, 18–19, 20–21, 26

Yōrō Code, 22

Yoshino, 61

Za, 79

The text of this book was set on the Linotype in Garamond (No. 3), a modern rendering of the type first cut by Claude Garamond (1510–1561). Garamond was a pupil of Geoffroy Troy and is believed to have based his letters on the Venetian models, although he introduced a number of important differences, and it is to him we owe the letter which we know as old-style. He gave to his letters a certain elegance and a feeling of movement that won for their creator an immediate reputation and the patronage of Francis I of France.

Composed, printed, and bound by The Colonial Press Inc., Clinton, Massachusetts. Typography and cover design by Elton Robinson. Cover map by J. P. Tremblay.